A Bibliography of the

Personal Computer

A Bibliography of the

Personal Computer

The Books and Periodical Articles

Roy A. Allan

Allan Publishing
London, Ontario, Canada.

First Edition 1.0

Library and Archives Canada Cataloguing in Publication

Allan, Roy A., 1931-
A bibliography of the personal computer: the books and periodical articles / Roy A. Allan.

ISBN 0-9689108-4-X

1. Microcomputers--Bibliography. I. Title.

Z5643.M48A55 2005   016.00416   C2005-900534-3

Additional copies or more information on the book are available from: Allan Publishing, 1624 Louise Blvd., London, Ontario, Canada. N6G 2R3

Printed and bound in the United States.

This book is dedicated to my daughters Jackie, Lisa and Susan; my sons Scott and Thomas; and my dear wife Ann Louise.

Contents

Preface

This bibliography has been abstracted from my book entitled "A History of the Personal Computer: The People and the Technology" (ISBN 0-9689108-0-7). It has been updated to add additional books and new books released between 2001 and 2005. It has also been rearranged to facilitate its use as a separate publication.

Part One of the book is a bibliography of books and Part Two is a bibliography of periodical articles.

We do believe that this bibliography is the most extensive available in reference to the history of the personal computer and the industry. The author would appreciate advisement of any errors or omissions.

Part Three is a reprint of an article written by the author entitled "What Was The First Personal Computer?" It was first printed in *The Analytical Engine*, May 1996 issue, Volume 3.3, pp. 42-46, a Journal of the Computer History Association of California. The reprint has been adjusted to correct an editorial error noted in the Fall 1996 issue, page 33 of the journal. This journal was discontinued after the Fall 1996 issue.

Roy A. Allan,

London, Ontario, Canada

March, 2005.

Part One: BOOKS

Personal Computing and Computers.

Allan, Roy A.
A History of the Personal Computer: The People and the Technology.
London, Canada: Allan Publishing, 2001.
Bardini, Thierry.
Bootstrapping: Douglas Engelbart, Coevolution, and the Origins of Personal Computing.
Stanford: Stanford University Press, 2000.
Clark, W.A. and C.E. Molnar.
A Description of the LINC.
In *"Computers in Biomedical Research Corporation."*
Editors: Ralph W. Stacy and Bruce D. Waxman.
New York: Academic Press, 1965; Chap. 2.
Evans, Christopher.
The Making of the Micro: A History of the Computer.
London, England: Victor Gollancz, 1981.
-- The "Micro" in the title refers to the microprocessor. The book does not contain any history of the microcomputer. The author died in 1979 prior to completion of the book, which was finished by Tom Stonier.
Freiberger, Paul and Michael Swaine.
Fire in the Valley: The Making of the Personal Computer.
Berkeley, Calif.: Osborne/McGraw-Hill, 1984.
-- A second edition was published by McGraw-Hill in 2000 that has been updated, with expanded coverage and numerous photographs.

Goldberg, Adele (Editor).
A History of Personal Workstations.
New York: ACM Press, 1988.
Gupta, Amar and Hoo-min D. Toong (Editors).
Insights Into Personal Computers.
New York: IEEE Engineers Press, 1985.
-- The book has "placed a heavy emphasis on technical depth and clarity."
Kemeny, John G.
Man and the Computer.
New York: Charles Scribner's Sons, 1972.
-- Has a chapter describing Dartmouth Time Sharing System.
Laing, Gordon.
DIGITAL RETRO: The Evolution and Design of the Personal Computer.
Alameda CA: Sybex, Inc., 2004.
McCarthy, John.
Time-Sharing Computer Systems.
In: *"Management and the Computer of the Future".*
Greenberger, Martin (Editor).
New York: MIT Press and John Wiley, 1962, pp. 220-248.
Osborne, Adam.
An Introduction to Microcomputers.   3 Vols.
Berkeley Calif.: Osborne/McGraw-Hill, 1977.
Pournelle, Jerry.
The Users Guide to Small Computers.
New York: Baen Books, 1984.
Veit, Stan.
Stan Veit's History of the Personal Computer: From Altair to IBM, A History of the PC Revolution.
Asheville, N.C.: WorldComm, 1993.
Waldrop, M. Mitchell.
The Dream Machine: J.C.R. Licklider and the Revolution That Made Computing Personal.
New York: Viking Press, 2001.

Apple Computer

Amelio, Gil and William L. Simon.
On the Firing Line: My 500 Days at Apple.
New York: HarperBusiness, 1998.
Brashares, Ann.
Steve Jobs: Thinks Different.
Brookfield, Connecticut: Millbrook Press, 2001.
-- A juvenile book for young readers.
Butcher, Lee.
Accidental Millionaire: The Rise and Fall of Steve Jobs at Apple Computer.
New York: Paragon House, 1988.
Carlton, Jim.
Apple: The Inside Story.
New York: Random House, 1997.
Deutschman, Alan.
The Second Coming of Steve Jobs.
New York: Broadway Books, 2000.
Gaines, Ann Graham.
Steve Jobs (Real-Life Reader Biography).
Hockessin, DE.: Mitchell Lane Publishers, 2000.
-- A juvenile book for young readers.
Garr, Doug.
Woz: The Prodigal Son of Silicon Valley.
New York: Avon Books, 1984.
Gassée, Jean-Louis.
The Third Apple: Personal Computers and the Cultural Revolution.
Orlando, Florida: Harcourt Brace Jovanovich, 1985.
Greenberg, Keith Elliot.
Steven Jobs & Stephen Wozniak: Creating the Apple Computer.
Woodbridge, Conn.: Blackbirch Press, 1994.
-- A juvenile book for young readers.
Hertzfeld, Andy.
Revolution in The Valley.
Sebastopol, Calif.: O'Reilly & Associates, 2004.

Kahney, Leander.
The Cult of Mac.
San Francisco, Calif.: No Starch Press, 2004.
Kawasaki, Guy.
The Macintosh Way.
New York: HarperPerennial, 1990.
Kelby, Scott.
Macintosh...the Naked Truth.
Indianapolis, Ind.: New Riders Publishing, 2002.
Kendall, Martha E.
Steve Wozniak: Inventor of the Apple Computer.
New York: Walker & Co., 1994.
-- A juvenile book for young readers.
Kunkel, Paul.
AppleDesign: The Work of the Apple Industrial Design Group.
New York: Graphics Inc., 1997.
LeVitus, Bob and Michael Fraase.
Guide to the Macintosh Underground: Mac Culture From the Inside.
Indianapolis, In.: Hayden Books, 1993.
Levy, Steven.
Insanely Great: The Life and Times of Macintosh, the Computer That Changed Everything.
New York: Viking, 1994.
Linzmayer, Owen W.
The Mac Bathroom Reader.
Alameda, Calif.: Sybex, 1994.
Linzmayer, Owen W.
Apple Confidential: The Real Story of Apple Computer, Inc.
San Francisco, Calif.: No Starch Press, 1999.
Linzmayer, Owen W.
Apple Confidential 2.0: The Definitive History of the World's Most Colorful Company.
San Francisco, Calif.: No Starch Press, 2004.

Malone, Michael S.
Infinite Loop: How Apple, the World's Most Insanely Great Computer Company went Insane.
New York: Doubleday, 1999.

Menuez, Doug, Marcos Kounalakis and Paul Saffo.
Defying Gravity: The Making of Newton.
Hillsboro, Oregon: Beyond Words Publishing, 1993.
-- A photo-journalistic depiction of the Newton development.

Moritz, Michael.
The Little Kingdom: The Private Story of Apple Computer.
New York: William Morrow, 1984.

Owad, Tom.
Apple I Replica Creation: Back to the Garage.
Sebastopol, Calif.: Syngress/O'Reilly Publishing, 2005.

Price, Rob.
So Far: The First Ten Years of a Vision.
Cupertino, Calif.: Apple Computer, Inc., 1987.

Rose, Frank.
West of Eden: The End of Innocence at Apple Computer.
New York: Viking, 1989.

Rozakis, Laurie.
Steven Jobs: Computer Genius.
Vero Beach, Florida: Rourke Enterprises, 1993.
-- A juvenile book for young readers.

Schmucker, Kurt J.
The Complete Book of LISA.
New York: Harper & Row, 1984.

Sculley, John with John A. Byrne.
Odyssey: Pepsi to Apple ... A Journey of Adventure, Ideas and the Future.
New York: Harper & Row, 1987

Thygeson, Gordon.
Apple T-Shirts: A Yearbook of History at Apple Computer.
Scotts Valley, Calif.: Pomo Publishing, 1998.

Various.
Maclopedia: The ultimate reference on everything Macintosh!
Indianapolis, In.: Hayden Books, 1996.

Weyhrich, Steven.
Apple II History.
Self Published, Zonker Software, 1991.
Wilson, Susan.
Steve Jobs: Wizard of Apple Computer.
Springfield, New Jersey: Enslow Publishers, 2001.
-- A juvenile book for young readers.
Young, Jeffrey S.
Steve Jobs: The Journey is the Reward.
Glenview, Illinois: Scott, Foresman, 1988.
Young, Jeffrey S. and William L. Simon.
iCon Steve Jobs: The Greatest Second Act in the History of Business.
New York: John Wiley & Sons, 2005.

IBM

Carroll, Paul.
Big Blues: The Unmaking of IBM.
New York: Crown Publishers, 1993.
Chposky, James and Ted Leonis.
Blue Magic: The People, Power and Politics Behind The IBM Personal Computer.
New York: Facts on File Publications, 1988.
Dell, Deborah A. and F. Gerry Purdy.
ThinkPad: A Different Shade of Blue: Building A Successful IBM Brand.
Indianapolis: Sams (A Division of Macmillan Computer Publishing), 1999.
Ferguson, Charles H. and Charles R. Morris.
Computer Wars: The Fall of IBM and the Future of Global Technology.
New York: Random House, 1993.
Garr, Doug.
IBM Redux: Lou Gerstner & the Business Turnaround of the Decade.
New York: HarperBusiness, 1999.
Gerstner, Louis V.
Who Says Elephants Can't Dance?: Inside IBM's Historic Turnaround.
New York: HarperBusiness, 2002.
Heller, Robert.
The Fate of IBM.
London, England: Little, Brown and Company (UK), 1994.
Slater, Robert.
Saving Big Blue: Leadership Lessons & Turnaround Tactics of IBM's Lou Gerstner.
New York: McGraw-Hill, 1999.

Software

Birnes, William J. (Editor).
Personal Computer Programming Encyclopedia.
New York: McGraw-Hill, 1989.
Brooks, Frederick P.
The Mythical Man-Month: Essays on Software Engineering.
Reading, Mass.: Addison-Wesley, 1975.
Gosling, James., David S.H. Rosenthal, and Michele J. Arden.
The NeWS Book: An Introduction to the Network/extensible Window System.
New York: Springer-Verlag, 1989.
-- Chapter 3 has a history of Windows development with an emphasis on the relationship to Sun workstations.
Grauer, Robert T. and Paul K. Sugrue.
Microcomputer Applications.
New York: McGraw-Hill, 1989.
Hoch, Detlev J., Cyriac R. Roeding, Gert Purkert, Sandro K. Linder with Ralph Müller.
Secrets of Software Success: Management Insights from 100 Software Firms Around the World.
Boston, Mass.: Harvard Business School Press, 1999.
Hsu, Jeffrey.
Microcomputer Programming Languages.
Hasbrouck Heights, N.J.: Hayden Book Co, 1986.
Kemeny, John G. and Thomas E. Kurtz.
Back to BASIC: The History, Competition, and Future of the Language.
Reading, Mass.: Addison-Wesley, 1985.
Moody, Glyn.
Rebel Code: The Inside Story of Linux and the Open Source Revolution.
Cambridge, Mass.: Perseus Publishing, 2001.
Nietz, Kerry.
FoxTales: Behind the Scenes at Fox Software.
Whitefish Bay, WI: Hentzenwerke Publishing, 2003.

Raymond, Eric S.
The Cathedral & the Bazaar: Musings on Linux and Open Source by an Accidental Revolutionary.
Sebastopol, Calif.: O'Reilly & Associates, 1999.
-- A history of hackers and the development of open-source software.
Torvalds, Linus and David Diamond.
Just for Fun: The Story of an Accidental Revolutionary.
New York: HarperBusiness, 2001.
-- Autobiography of Linus Torvalds and his creation of the Linux operating system.
Wayner, Peter.
Free For All: How Linux and the Free Software Movement Undercut the High-Tech Titans.
New York: HarperBusiness, 2000.

Microsoft

Andrews, Paul.
*How the Web Was Won: Microsoft from Windows to the Web:
The Inside Story of How Bill Gates and His Band of Internet
Idealists Transformed a Software Empire.*
New York: Broadway Books, 1999.
Auletta, Ken.
World War 3.0: Microsoft and its Enemies.
New York: Random House, 2001.
Bank, David.
*Breaking Windows: How Bill Gates Fumbled the Future of
Microsoft.*
New York: The Free Press, 2001.
Barr, Adam.
*Proudly Serving My Corporate Masters: What I Learned in Ten
Years as a Microsoft Programmer.*
Lincoln, NE.: Writers Club Press, 2000.
Bick, Julie.
All I really Need to Know in Business I Learned at Microsoft.
New York: Pocket Books, 1997.
-- A personal guide to business management.
Boyd, Aaron.
Smart Money: The Story of Bill Gates.
Greensboro, N.C.: Morgan Reynolds, 1995.
-- A juvenile book for young readers.
Brinkley, Joel and Steve Lohr.
U.S. V. Microsoft: The Inside Story of the Landmark Case.
New York: McGraw-Hill, 2001.
Cusumano, Michael A. and Richard W. Selby.
*Microsoft Secrets: How the World's Most Powerful Software
Company Creates Technology, Shapes Markets, and Manages
People.*
New York: Free Press, 1995.
Dearlove, Des.
*Business the Bill Gates Way: 10 Secrets of the World's Richest
Business Leader.*
New York: Amacon, American Management Association, 1999.

Dickinson, Joan D.
Bill Gates: Billionaire Computer Genius.
Springfield, N.J.: Enslow Publishers, 1997.
-- A juvenile book for young readers.
Drummond, Michael.
Renegades of the Empire: A Tale of Success, Failures and Other Dark Deeds Inside Fortress Microsoft.
New York: Three Rivers Press, 1999.
Edstrom, Jennifer and Marlin Eller.
Barbarians Led by Bill Gates -- Microsoft from the Inside: How the World's Richest Corporation Wields its Power.
New York: Henry Holt and Company, 1998.
Ferry, Steven.
The Building of Microsoft.
Mankato, MN.: Smart Apple Media, 1999.
Foreman, Michael.
Bill Gates, Software Billionaire.
Parsippany, NJ.: Crestwood House, 1999.
Gates, Bill with Nathan Myhrvold and Peter Rinearson.
The Road Ahead.
New York: Viking, 1995.
Gates, Bill with Collins Hemingway.
Business @ The Speed of Thought: Using a Digital Nervous System.
New York: Warner books, 1999.
Gatlin, Jonathan,
Bill Gates: The Path to the Future.
New York: Avon Books, 1999.
Heilemann, John.
Pride Before the Fall: The Trials of Bill Gates and the End of the Microsoft Era.
New York: HarperCollins, 2001.
Ichbiah, Daniel and Susan L. Knepper.
The Making of Microsoft.
Rocklin, Calif.: Prima Publishing, 1991.

Lewis, Ted G.
Microsoft Rising ... and other tales of Silicon Valley.
Los Alamitos, Calif.: IEEE Computer Society, 1999.
-- Mainly a reprint of *IEEE Computer* periodical articles, with minimal Microsoft content.
Liebowitz, Stan J. and Stephen E. Margolis.
Winners, Losers and Microsoft: Competition and Antitrust in High Technology.
Oakland, Calif.: The Independent Institute, 1999.
Lowe, Janet.
Bill Gates Speaks: Insight from the World's Greatest Entrepreneur.
New York: John Wiley & Sons, 1998.
Manes, Stephen and Paul Andrews.
Gates: How Microsoft's Mogul Reinvented an Industry and Made Himself The Richest Man in America.
New York: Doubleday, 1993.
Marshall, David.
Bill Gates and Microsoft.
Watford, England: Exley, 1994.
Maxwell, Fredric Alan.
Bad Boy Ballmer: The Man Who Rules Microsoft.
New York: William Morrow, 2002.
Microsoft Staff.
Inside Out! Microsoft – In our own words.
New York: Warner Books, 2000.
-- 25th Microsoft Anniversary book, 1975 – 2000.
Moody, Fred.
I Sing the Body Electronic: A Year with Microsoft on the Multimedia Frontier.
New York: Viking, 1995.
Rich, Laura.
The Accidental Zillionaire: Demystifying Paul Allen.
Hoboken, NJ.: John Wiley & Sons, 2003.
Rivlin, Gary.
The Plot to Get Bill Gates: An Irreverent Investigation of the World's Richest Man...and the People Who Hate Him.
New York: Times Business/Random House, 1999.

Rohm, Wendy Goldman.
The Microsoft File: The Secret Case Against Bill Gates.
New York: Times Business/Random House, 1998.
Slater, Robert.
Microsoft Rebooted: How Bill Gates and Steve Ballmer Reinvented Their Company.
New York: Penguin Group, 2004.
Stross, Randall E.
The Microsoft Way: The Real Story of How the Company Outsmarts Its Competition.
Reading, Mass.: Addison-Wesley, 1996.
Tsang, Cheryl D.
Microsoft First Generation: The Success Secrets of the Visionaries Who Launched a Technological Empire.
New York: John Wiley & Sons, 1999.
Wallace, James and Jim Erickson.
Hard Drive: Bill Gates and the Making of the Microsoft Empire.
New York: John Wiley & Sons, 1992.
Wallace, James.
Overdrive: Bill Gates and the Race to Control Cyberspace.
New York: John Wiley & Sons, 1997.
Woog, Adam.
Bill Gates.
San Diego: Lucent Books, 1999.
Zachary, G. Pascal.
Show-Stopper! The Breakneck Race to Create Windows NT and the Next Generation at Microsoft.
New York: Free Press, 1994.

Companies, Organizations & People

Adamson, Ian and Richard Kennedy.
Sinclair and the 'Sunrise' Technology.
Harmondsworth, England: Penguin Books, 1986.
Anders, George.
Perfect Enough: Carly Fiorina and the Reinvention of Hewlett-Packard.
Mew York: Portfolia/Penguin Group, 2003.
Angel, Karen.
Inside Yahoo!: Reinvention and the Road Ahead.
New York: John Wiley & Sons, 2002.
Brockman, John.
DIGERATI: Encounters with the Cyber Elite.
San Francisco, Calif.: HardWired, 1996.
Bronson, Po.
The Nudist on the Late Shift: and Other True Tales of Silicon Valley.
New York: Random House, 1999.
Brown, Kenneth A.
Inventors at Work: Interviews with 16 Notable American Inventors.
Redmond, Washington: Tempus Books, 1988.
-- Includes interviews with Marcian E. "Ted" Hoff and Steve Wozniak.
Buderi, Robert.
Engines of Tomorrow: How the World's Best Companies Are Using Their Research Labs to Win the Future.
New York: Simon & Schuster, 2000.
Bunnell, David with Adam Brate.
Making the CISCO Connection: The Story Behind the Real Internet Superpower.
New York: John Wiley & Sons, 2000.
Burrows, Peter.
Backfire: Carly Fiorina's High-Stakes Battle for the Soul of Hewlett-Packard.
Hoboken NJ.: John Wiley & Sons, 2003.

Butter, Andrea and David Pogue.
Piloting Palm: The Inside Story of Palm, Handspring, and the Birth of the Billion-Dollar Handheld Industry.
New York: John Wiley & Sons, 2002.

Caddes, Carolyn.
Portraits of Success: Impressions of Silicon Valley Pioneers.
Palo Alto, Calif.: Tioga Publishing, 1986.

Carlston, Douglas G.
Software People: An Insider's Look at the Personal Computer Software Industry.
New York: Simon & Schuster, 1985.

Cassidy, John.
dot.con: The Greatest Story Ever Told.
New York: HarperCollins, 2002.

Clark, Jim with Owen Edwards.
Netscape Time: The Making of the Billion-Dollar Start-Up That Took On Microsoft
New York: St. Martin's Press, 1999.

Cohen, Adam.
the Perfect Store: Inside EBAY.
New York: Little, Brown & Co., 2002.

Cohen, Scott.
Zap! The Rise and Fall of Atari.
New York: McGraw-Hill, 1984.

Cringely, Robert X.
Accidental Empires: How the Boys of Silicon Valley Make Their Millions, Battle Foreign Competition, and Still Can't Get a Date.
Reading, Mass.: Addison-Wesley, 1992.

Cusumano, Michael A. and David B. Yoffie.
Competing On Internet Time: Lessons from Netscape and Its Battle with Microsoft.
New York: The Free Press/Simon & Schuster, 1998.

Dale, Rodney.
The Sinclair Story.
London, England: Duckworth & Co, 1985.

Datapro Research.
Who's Who in Microcomputing 1984-85.
Delran, N.J.: Datapro Research Corporation, 1984.

Dell, Michael with Catherine Fredman.
Direct from Dell: Strategies That Revolutionized an Industry.
New York: HarperBusiness, 1999.
Editors (Senior): George Sutton, James R. Talbot and Alan Chai.
Hoover's Guide to Computer Companies: 2nd Edition.
Austin, Texas: Hoover's Business Press, 1996.
Ehrbar, Al.
The Verbatim Story: The First Twenty-Five Years.
Lyme, Conn.: Greenwich Publishing Group, 1995.
Grossman, Wendy M. (Editor).
Remembering the Future: Interviews from Personal Computer World.
London, England: Springer-Verlag, 1997.
-- A collection of articles previously published in the British magazine *Personal Computer World.*
Hall, Mark and John Barry.
Sunburst: The Ascent of Sun Microsystems.
Chicago, Illinois: Contemporary Books, 1990.
Hiltzik, Michael.
Dealers of Lightning: XEROX PARC and the Dawn of the Computer.
New York: HarperBusiness, 1999.
Jager, Rama D. and Rafael Ortiz.
In the Company of Giants: Candid Conversations with the Visionaries of the Digital World.
New York: McGraw-Hill, 1997.
James, Geoffrey.
Success Secrets from Silicon Valley: How to make your teams more effective.
Formerly Titled:
Business Wisdom of the Electronic Elite
New York: Time Business/Random House, 1998.
-- A business management guide.
Jessen, Kenneth Christian.
How it All Began: Hewlett-Packard's Loveland Facility.
Loveland, CO.: J.V. Publications, 1999.

Kaplan, David A.
The Silicon Boys: and Their Valley of Dreams.
New York: William Morrow & Co, 1999.
Kaplan, Jerry.
Startup: A Silicon Valley Adventure.
New York: Houghton Mifflin, 1995.
Kenney, Charles C.
Riding The Runaway Horse: The Rise and Decline of Wang.
Boston: Little, Brown and Company, 1992.
-- Has a chapter on "The Personal Computer Revolution."
Kenney, Martin and John Seely Brown (Editors).
Understanding Silicon Valley: The Anatomy of an Entrepreneurial Region.
Stanford: Stanford University Press, 2000.
Klein, Alec.
Stealing Time: Steve Case, Jerry Levin, and the Collapse of AOL Time Warner.
New York: Simon & Schuster, 2003.
Lammers, Susan.
Programmers at Work: Interviews with 19 Programmers Who Shaped the Computer Industry.
Redmond, Washington: Tempus Books, 1986.
Laver, Ross.
Random Excess: The Wild Ride of Michael Cowpland and Corel.
New York: Viking, 1998.
Lee, J.A.N.
Computer Pioneers.
IEEE Computer Society Press, 1995.
Levering, Robert., Michael Katz and Milton Moskowitz.
The Computer Entrepreneurs: Who's Making it Big and How in America's Upstart Industry.
New York: Nal Books, 1984.
Levy, Steven.
Hackers: Heroes of the Computer Revolution.
New York: Doubleday/Anchor Press, 1984.

Lewis, Michael.
The New New Thing: A Silicon Valley Story.
New York: Norton & Company, 1999.
-- A biographical story of Jim Clark (Silicon Graphics and Netscape).
Littman, Jonathan.
Once Upon a Time in ComputerLand: The Amazing, Billion Dollar Tale of Bill Millard's ComputerLand Empire.
Los Angeles, Calif.: Price Stern Sloan, 1987.
Mahon, Thomas.
Charged Bodies: People Power and Paradox in Silicon Valley.
New York: Nal Books, 1985.
Malone, Michael S.
The Big Score: The Billion-Dollar Story of Silicon Valley.
New York: Doubleday, 1985.
Osborne, Adam and John Dvorak.
Hypergrowth: The Rise and Fall of Osborne Computer Corporation.
Berkeley, Calif.: Idthekkethan Publishing, 1984.
Packard, David.
The HP Way: How Bill Hewlett and I Built Our Company.
New York: HarperBusiness, 1995.
Pearson, Jamie Parker (Editor).
Digital at Work: Snapshots from the first thirty-five years.
Burlington, Mass.: Digital Press, 1992.
Peterson, W.E. Pete.
AlmostPerfect: How a Bunch of Regular Guys Built WordPerfect Corporation.
Rocklin, Calif.: Prima Publishing, 1994.
Pfiffner, Pamela.
Inside the Publishing Revolution: The Adobe Story.
Berkeley, CA.: Peachpit Press, 2003.
Quittner, Joshua and Michelle Slatalla.
Speeding the Net: The Inside Story of Netscape and How it Challenged Microsoft.
New York: Atlantic Press, 1998.

Read, Stuart.
The Oracle Edge: How Oracle Corporation's Take-No- Prisoners Strategy Has Created an $8 Billion Software Powerhouse.
Holbrook, Mass.: Adams Media, 1999.
-- Mainly a business management text.

Rifkin, Glenn and George Harrar.
The Ultimate Entrepreneur: The Story of Ken Olsen and Digital Equipment Corporation.
Chicago, Illinois: Contemporary Books, 1988.

Schein, Edgar H.
DEC is Dead, Long Live DEC: The Lasting Legacy of the Digital Equipment Corporation.
San Francisco: Berre Koehler Publications, 2003.

Schroeder, Katherine and Suzanne E. Taylor.
Inside Intuit: How the Makers of Quicken Beat Microsoft and Revolutionized an Entire Industry.
Boston: Harvard Business School Press, 2003.

Sigismund, Charles G.
Champions of Silicon Valley: Visionary Thinking from Today's Technology Pioneers.
New York: John Wiley & Sons, 2000.

Slater, Robert.
Portraits in Silicon.
Cambridge, Mass.: MIT Press, 1989.

Slater, Robert.
The Eye of the Storm: How John Chambers Steered Cisco Through the Technology Collapse.
New York: HarperBusiness, 2003.

Smith, Douglas K. and Robert C. Alexander.
Fumbling The Future: How Xerox Invented, Then Ignored, The First Personal Computer.
New York: William Morrow, 1988.

Southwick, Karen.
Silicon Gold Rush: The Next Generation of High-Tech Stars Rewrites the Rules of Business.
New York: John Wiley & Sons, 1999.
-- A business management book about the high-tech industry.

Southwick, Karen.
   *High Noon: The Inside Story of Scott McNealy and the Rise of
   Sun Microsystems.*
   New York: John Wiley & Sons, 1999.
Spector, Robert.
   amazon.com: Get Big Fast.
   New York: HarperBusiness, 2000.
Spencer, Donald D.
   Great Men and Women of Computing, 2nd Edition.
   Ormond beach, Florida: Camelot, 1999.
Stross, Randall E.
   Steve Jobs & The NeXT Big Thing.
   New York: Atheneum, 1993.
Stross, Randall E.
   eBoys: The First Inside Account of Venture Capitalists at Work.
   New York: Crown Business, 2000.
Swisher, Kara.
   *aol.com: How Steve Case Beat Bill Gates, Nailed the Netheads,
    and Made Millions in the War for the Web.*
   New York: Random House/Time Books, 1998.
Symonds, Matthew.
   Softwar: An Intimate Portrait of Larry Ellison and Oracle.
   New York: Simon & Schuster, 2003.
Texas Instruments.
   *50 Years of Innovation: The History of Texas Instruments
    -- A Story of people and their ideas.*
   Dallas, Texas: Texas Instruments, 1980.
   -- A company publication.
Thomas, David.
   *Knights of the New Technology: The Inside Story of Canada's
   Computer Elite.*
   Toronto, Canada: Key Porter Books, 1983.
Tomczyk, Michael S.
   *The Home Computer Wars: An Insider's Account of Commodore
    and Jack Tramiel.*
   Greensboro, North Carolina: Compute! Publications, 1984.

Voyer, Roger and Patti Ryan.
  *The New Innovators: How Canadians Are Shaping the Knowledge
    Based Economy.*
  Toronto, Canada: James Lorimer, 1994.
Waters, John K.
  *John Chambers and the CISCO Way: Navigating Through
    Volatility.*
  New York: John Wiley & Sons, 2002.
Wilson, Mike.
  *The Difference Between God and Larry Ellison: Inside Oracle
    Corporation.*
  New York: William Morrow, 1997.
Young, Jeffrey.
  *Forbes Greatest Technology Stories: Inspiring Tales of the
    Entrepreneurs and Inventors Who Revolutionized Modern
    Business.*
  New York: John Wiley & Sons, 1998.
Young, Jeffrey S.
  *CISCO UnAuthorized: Inside the High-Stakes Race to Own the
    Future.*
  Roseville, CA.: Forum, Prima Publishing, 2001.
Young, Robert and Wendy Rohm.
  *Under the Radar: How Red Hat Changed the Software Business
    -- and Took Microsoft by Surprise.*
  Scottsdale, Arizona: Coriolis Group, 1999.

Miscellaneous

Ahl, David H. (Editor).
The Best of Creative Computing: Volumes 1 and 2.
Morristown, New Jersey: Creative Computing Press,6 1976.
-- Vol. 1 consists of material from the first six issues.
Ahl, David H. and Carl T. Helmers, Jr. (Editors).
The Best of Byte: Volume 1.
Morristown, New Jersey: Creative Computing Press, 1977.
-- Includes material from the first twelve issues.
Augarten, Stan.
BIT by BIT: An Illustrated History of Computers.
New York: Ticknor & Fields, 1984.
Bowker, R.R.
Microcomputer Market Place 1985: A Comprehensive Directory of the Microcomputer Industry.
New York: R.R. Bowker, 1985.
Campbell-Kelly, Martin and William Aspray.
Computer: A History of the Information Machine.
New York: BasicBooks, 1996.
Ditlea, Steve (Editor).
DIGITAL DELI: The comprehensive, user-lovable menu of computer lore, culture, lifestyles and fancy.
New York: Workman Publishing, 1984.
Durbeck, Robert C. and Sol Sherr.
Output Hardcopy Devices.
San Diego, Calif.: Academic Press, 1988.
Dvorak, John C.
Dvorak Predicts: An Insider's Look at the Computer Industry.
Berkeley, California: Osborne/McGraw-Hill, 1994.
-- The book is now somewhat dated and parts of the book appeared in various periodicals.
Dyson, Esther
Release 2.0: A design for living in the digital age.
New York: Broadway Books, 1997.
Finn, Christine.
Artifacts: An Archaelogist's Year in Silicon Valley.
Cambridge, MA.: MIT Press, 2001.

Glass, Robert L.
Computing Calamities: Lessons Learned from Products, Projects, and Companies that Failed.
Upper Saddle River, N.J.: Prentice Hall PTR, 1999.
-- Contains information on problems at companies such as Atari, Commodore, Novell and Wang.
Goody, Roy W.
The Intelligent Microcomputer.
Chicago, Illinois: Science Research Associates, 1986.
Greelish, David.
Historically Brewed: Our First Year.
Jacksonville, Florida: HCS Press, 1994.
Haddock, Dr. Thomas F.
A Collector's Guide To Personal Computers and Pocket Calculators.
Florence, Alabama: Books Americana, 1993.
Hanson, Dirk.
The New Alchemists: Silicon Valley and the Microelectronics Revolution.
Boston, Mass.: Little, Brown and Company, 1982.
Hyman, Michael.
PC Roadkill.
Foster City, Calif.: IDG Books, 1995.
Kidder, Tracy.
The Soul of a New Machine.
New York: Avon Books, 1981.
Kidwell, Peggy A. and Paul E. Ceruzzi.
Landmarks in Digital Computing: A Smithsonian Pictorial History.
Washington, D.C.: Smithsonian Institution Press, 1994.
Koblentz, Evan.
Guide to U.S. Computer Museums.
Springfield, NJ: Self-published, 2004.
Markoff, John.
What the Dormouse Said: How the 60s Counterculture Shaped the Personal Computer.
New York: Viking Adult, 2005.

Mims, Forrest M. III.
Siliconnections: Coming of Age in the Electronic Era.
New York: McGraw-Hill, 1986.
Nadeau, Michael.
Collectible Microcomputers.
Atglen, PA.: Schiffer Publishing, 2002.
Negroponte, Nicholas.
being digital.
New York: Knopf, Inc., 1995.
Nelson, Theodor H.
Computer Lib and Dream Machines.
South Bend, In.: Self Published in 1974.
Nyce, James M. and Paul Kahn (Editors).
From Memex to Hypertext: Vannevar Bush and the Mind's Machine.
San Diego, Calif.: Academic Press, 1991.
Osborne, Adam.
Running Wild: The Next Industrial Revolution.
Berkeley, Calif.: Osborne/McGraw-Hill, 1979
Palfreman, Jon and Doron Swade.
The Dream Machine: Exploring the Computer Age.
London, England: BBC Books, 1991.
-- The book is derived from a television mini-series.
Ranade, Jay and Alan Nash (Editors).
The Best of BYTE: Two decades on the Leading Edge.
New York: McGraw-Hill, 1994.
Rogers, Everett M. and Judith K. Larsen.
Silicon Valley Fever: Growth of High Technology Culture.
New York: Basic Books, 1984.
Shirinian, George.
Microcomputing Periodicals: An Annotated Directory.
Toronto, Canada: George Shirinian, 1985.
Stork, David G. (Editor).
HAL's Legacy: 2001's Computer as Dream and Reality.
Cambridge, Mass.: MIT Press, 1997.

Stumpf, Kevin.
*A Guide to Collecting Computers and Computer Collectibles:
History Practice and Techniques.*
Kitchener, Ontario, Canada: Self published, 1998.

Microprocessors

Byman, Jeremy.
Andrew Grove and the Intel Corporation.
Greensboro, NC: Morgan Reynolds, 1999.
Jackson, Tim.
*Inside Intel: Andy Grove and the Rise of the World's Most
Powerful Chip Company.*
New York: Dutton, 1997.
Kaye, Glynnis Thompson (Editor).
A Revolution in Progress: A History of Intel to Date.
Santa Clara, Calif.: Intel Corporation, 1984.
Malone, Michael S.
The Microprocessor: A Biography.
New York: Springer-Verlag, 1995.
Noyce, Robert N. and Marcian E. Hoff.
A History of Microprocessor Development at Intel.
Santa Clara, Calif.: Intel Corp., Public AR-173.
Smolan, Rick and Jennifer Erwitt.
One Digital Day: How the Microchip is Changing Our World.
New York: Times Books/Random House, 1998.
-- The book was sponsored by the Intel Corporation. It is a
photographic documentation of the microprocessor's vast
influence world-wide.
YU, Albert.
*Creating the Digital Future: the Secrets of Consistent Innovation
at Intel.*
New York: Free Press, 1998.
Zygmont, Jeffrey.
Microchip: An Idea, Its Genesis, and the Revolution It Created.
Cambridge, MA: Perseus Publishing, 2003.

Internet and the World Wide Web

Abbate, Janet.
Inventing the Internet.
Cambridge: MIT Press, 1999.
Berners-Lee, Tim with Mark Fischetti
Weaving the Web: The Original Design and Ultimate Destiny of the WORLD WIDE WEB by its Inventor.
New York: Harper San Francisco, 1999.
Ferguson, Charles H.
High St@kes, No Prisoners: A Winner's Tale of Greed and Glory in the Internet Wars.
New York: Time Books, 1999.
Hafner, Katie and John Markoff.
Cyberpunk: Outlaws and Hackers on the Computer Frontier.
New York: Simon & Schuster, 1991.
-- Stories of three hackers who create havoc on computer networks.
Hafner, Katie and Lyon, Mathew.
Where Wizards Stay Up Late: The Origins of the Internet.
New York: Simon & Schuster, 1996.
Jefferis, David.
Cyber Space: Virtual Reality and the World Wide Web.
New York: Crabtree Pub., 1999.
Metcalfe, Bob.
Internet Collapses and Other InfoWorld Punditry.
Foster City, CA.: IDG Books Worldwide, 2000.
-- A collection of columns from InfoWorld periodical.
Naughton, John.
A Brief History of the Future: The Origins and Destiny of the Internet.
London: Weidenfeld & Nicolson, 1999.
Randall, Neil.
The Soul of the Internet: Net Gods, Netizens and The Wiring of the World.
London, United Kingdom: International Thomson Computer Press, 1997.

Reid, Robert H.
Architects of the Web: 1000 Days that Built the Future of Business.
New York: John Wiley & Sons, 1997.

Salus, Peter H.
Casting the Net: From ARPANET to Internet and Beyond.
Reading, Mass.: Addison-Wesley, 1995.

Segaller, Stephen.
NERDS 2.0.1: A Brief History of the Internet
New York: TV Books, 1998.
-- A companion book to the PBS television series of the same title.

Stauffer, David.
Business the AOL Way: Secrets of the World's Most Successful Web Company.
Oxford: Capstone, 2000.

Stoll, Clifford.
Silicon Snake Oil: Second Thoughts on the Information Highway.
New York: Doubleday, 1995.

Wolinsky, Art.
The History of the Internet and the World Wide Web.
Springfield, New Jersey: Enslow Publishers, 1999.

Reference

Allan, Roy A.
A Bibliography of the Personal Computer: The Books and Periodical Articles.
London, Canada: Allan Publishing, 2005.
Bowker, R.R.
Bowker's Complete Sourcebook of Personal Computing 1985.
New York: R.R. Bowker, 1984.
Cortada, James W.
Historical Dictionary of Data Processing: Biographies.
Westport, Conn.: Greenwood Press, 1987.
Cortada, James W.
Historical Dictionary of Data Processing: Organizations.
Westport, Conn.: Greenwood Press, 1987.
Cortada, James W.
Historical Dictionary of Data Processing: Technology.
Westport, Conn.: Greenwood Press, 1987.
Cortada, James W.
A Bibliographic Guide to the History of Computing, Computers, and the Information Processing Industry.
Westport, Conn.: Greenwood Press, 1990.
Cortada, James W.
A Bibliographic Guide to the History of Computer Applications, 1950-1990.
Westport, Conn.: Greenwood Press, 1996.
Editors of *The Red Herring* periodical.
The Red Herring Guide to the Digital Universe: The inside look at the technology business – from Silicon Valley to Hollywood.
New York: Warner Books, 1996.
Glossbrenner, Alfred and Emily.
Computer Sourcebook.
New York: Random House, 1977.
Juliussen, Egil, Portia Isaacson and Luanne Kruse (Editors).
Computer Industry Almanac.
Dallas, Texas: Computer Industry Almanac, 1987.

Kent, Allen and James G. Williams (Executive Editors).
  Encyclopedia of Microcomputers (Volumes 1 to 15).
  New York: Marcel Dekker, 1988/95.
Petska-Juliussen, Karen and Dr. Egil Juliussen.
  The 8th Annual Computer Industry Almanac.
  Austin, Texas: The Reference Press, 1996.
Sayre Van.
  *MicroSource: Where to Find Answers to Questions About
  Microcomputers.*
  Littleton, Colorado: Libraries Unlimited, 1986.

Early Computer Technology

The Original Digital Computers

Burkes, Alice R. and Arthur W. Burkes.
The First Electronic Computer.
Ann Arbor, Mich.: University of Michigan Press, 1989.
Ceruzzi, Paul E.
Reckoners: The Prehistory of the Digital Computer, from Relays to the Stored Program Concept, 1935-1945.
Westport, Conn.: Greenwood Press, 1983.
Ceruzzi, Paul E.
A History of Modern Computing.
Westport, Conn.: Greenwood Press, 1998.
-- Covers the transition to the microprocessor and personal computer.
Goldstine, Herman H.
The Computer from Pascal to von Neumann.
Princeton, N.J.: Princeton University Press, 1972.
Ifrah, Georges.
The Universal History of Computing: From the Abacus to the Quantum Computer.
New York: John Wiley & Sons, 2000.
Lavington, Simon S.
Early British Computers.
Manchester, England: Manchester University Press, 1980.
Lukoff, Herman.
From Dits To Bits: A Personal History of the Electronic Computer.
Portland, Oregon: Robotics Press, 1979.
Lundstrom, David E.
A Few Good Men from Univac
Cambridge, Mass.: MIT Press, 1987.

Metropolis, N., J. Howlet and Gian-Carlo Rota (Editors).
A History of Computing in the Twentieth Century.
New York: Academic Press, 1980.

Mollenhoff, Clark R.
Atanasoff: Forgotten Father of the Computer.
Ames, Iowa: Iowa State University Press, 1988.

Moreau, R.
The Computer Comes of Age: The People, the Hardware, and the Software.
Cambridge, Mass.: MIT Press, 1984.

Pylyshyn, Zenon W. (Editor).
Perspectives on the Computer Revolution.
Englewood Cliffs, N.J.: Prentice-Hall, 1970.

Randell, Brian.
The Origins of Digital Computers: Selected Papers.
New York: Springer-Verlag, 1975.

Redmond, Kent C. and Thomas M. Smith
Project Whirlwind: The History of a Pioneer Computer.
Bedford, Mass.: Digital Press, 1981.

Ritchie, David.
The Computer Pioneers: The Making of the Modern Computer.
New York: Simon & Schuster, 1986.

Shurkin, Joel.
Engines of the Mind: A History of the Computer.
New York: Norton & Company, 1984.

Stern, Nancy.
From Eniac to Univac: An Appraisal of the Eckert-Mauchly Computers.
Bedford, Mass.: Digital Press, 1981.

Wildes, Karl L. and Nilo A. Lindgren.
A Century of Electrical Engineering and Computer Science at MIT, 1882 - 1982.
Cambridge, Mass.: MIT Press, 1985.

Wilkes, Maurice.
Memoirs of a Computer Pioneer.
Cambridge, Mass.: MIT Press, 1985.

Williams, Michael R.
A History of Computing Technology.
Englewood Cliffs, N.J.: Prentice-Hall, 1985.

IBM

Bashe, Charles J., Lyle R. Johnson, John H. Palmer and Emerson W.
Pugh.
IBM's Early Computers.
Cambridge, Mass.: MIT Press, 1986.
Belden, Thomas and Marva Belden.
The Lengthening Shadow: The Life of Thomas J. Watson.
Boston, Mass.: Little, Brown and Company, 1962.
Pugh, Emerson W.
*Memories That Shaped An Industry: Decisions Leading to IBM
System/360.*
Cambridge, Mass.: MIT Press, 1984.
Pugh, Emerson W., Lyle R. Johnson and John H. Palmer.
IBM's 360 and Early 370 Systems.
Cambridge, Mass.: MIT Press, 1991.
Pugh, Emerson W.
Building IBM, Shaping an Industry and Its Technology.
Cambridge, Mass.: MIT Press, 1995.
Rodgers, William.
Think: A Biography of the Watsons and IBM.
New York: Stein and Day, 1969.
Watson, Thomas J. Jr.
A Business and Its Beliefs: The Ideas That Helped Build IBM.
New York: McGraw-Hill, 1963.
Watson, Thomas J. Jr. and Peter Petre.
Father Son & Co.: My Life at IBM and Beyond.
New York: Bantam Books, 1990.

Technology

Braun, Ernest and Stuart Macdonald.
Revolution in Miniature: The History and Impact of Semiconductor Electronics.
Cambridge, Mass.: Cambridge University Press, 1982 (2nd Edition).
Gilder, George.
Microcosm: The Quantum Revolution in Economics and Technology.
New York: Simon & Schuster, 1989.
-- "A prescient look inside the expanding universe of economic, social and technological possibilities within the world of the silicon chip."
Morris, P.R.
A History of the World Semiconductor Industry.
London, England: Peter Peregrinus, 1990.
Reid, T.R.
The Chip: How Two Americans Invented the Microchip and Launched a Revolution.
New York: Simon and Schuster, 1984.
Riordan, Michael and Lillian Hoddeson.
Crystal Fire: The Birth of the Information Age.
New York: W.W. Norton & Company, 1997.

Software

Rosen, Saul (Editor).
Programming Systems and Languages.
New York: McGraw-Hill, 1967.
Sammet, Jean E.
Programming Languages: History and Fundamentals.
Englewood Cliffs, N.J.: Prentice-Hall, 1969.
Wexelblat, Richard L. (Editor).
History of Programming Languages.
New York: Academic Press, 1981.

Part Two: Periodicals

This part is a historical reference source of selected periodical articles. The articles provide additional detailed information on personal computer developments. The product articles are generally an initial review of the product shortly after its introduction.

Personal Computing and Computers.

Ahl, David H.
"The First Decade of Personal Computing."
Creative Computing (November 1984), pp. 30-45.
Allan, Roy A.
"What Was The First Personal Computer?"
The Analytical Engine (Volume 3.3, May 1996), pp. 42-46.
Archer, Rowland.
"The HP-75 Portable Computer."
BYTE (September 1983), pp. 178-186.
Baker, Robert.
"Product Description: OSI."
Byte (January 1977), pp. 94-95.
Describes Ohio Scientific(OSI) models 300 & 400 microcomputer boards
Barbour, Dennis E.
"Users Report: The SOL-20."
BYTE (April 1978), pp. 126-130.
Buchholz, Werner (Editor).
"Was the First Microcomputer Built in France?"
Annals of the History of Computing (Vol.10, No.2, 1988), page 142.
-- Editor discusses Micral R2E microcomputer.
Bumpous, Robert.
"A User's Reaction to the SOL-10 Computer."
BYTE (January 1978), pp. 86-93.

BYTE Staff.
"The New Heathkit Computer Line."
BYTE (August 1977), pp. 86-88.

Ceruzzi, Paul.
"From Scientific Instrument to Everyday Appliance:
The Emergence of Personal Computers, 1970 -1977."
History and Technology (Vol. 13, No. 1, 1996), pp. 1-31.

Ciarcia, Steve.
"Try This Computer on for Size."
BYTE (March 1977), pp. 114-129
-- Describes Digital Group microcomputer.

Crosby, Kip.
"Dawn of the Micro: Intel's Intellecs."
The Analytical Engine (Jan. - Mar. 1994), pp. 11-14.

Dahmke, Mark.
"The Heath H-89 Computer."
BYTE (August 1980), pp. 46-56.

Dahmke, Mark.
"The Osborne 1."
BYTE (June 1982), pp. 348-362.

Dahmke, Mark.
"The Compaq Computer: A portable and affordable alternative to
the IBM Personal Computer."
BYTE (January 1983), pp. 30-36.

Dickerman, Harold.
The Commodore 8032 Business System."
BYTE (August 1982), pp. 366-376.

Editor.
"Early Small Computers."
Annals of the History of Computing (11, No. 1, 1989), pp. 53-54.
-- The editor discusses Kenbak computer.

Editors.
"Computer! Build this microcomputer yourself. Add it to the TV
Typewriter for a complete computer system of your own."
Radio-Electronics (July 1974), pp. 29-33.
-- Describes construction details of Mark-8 computer.

Fager, Roger and John Bohr.
   "The Kaypro II."
   BYTE (September 1983), pp. 212-224.
Fano, R.M. and F.J. Corbato.
   "TIME-SHARING ON COMPUTERS."
   Scientific American (September 1966), pp. 128-312.
Fiegel, Curtis.
   "What a Concept: A View of the Corvus Computer."
   BYTE (May 1983), pp. 134-150.
Fylstra, Dan.
   "User's Report: The PET 2001."
   BYTE (March 1978), pp. 114-127.
Fylstra, Dan.
   "The Radio Shack TRS-80: An Owner's Report."
   BYTE (April 1978), pp. 49-60.
Garland, Harry.
   "design innovations in personal computers."
   Computer (March 1977), pp. 24-27.
Garrett, Billy.
   "The Timex/Sinclair 1000."
   BYTE (January 1983), pp. 364-370
Gray, Stephen B.
   "Building Your Own Computer."
   Computers and Automation (December 1971), pp. 25-31.
Gray, Stephen B.
   "The Early Days of Personal Computers."
   Creative Computing (November 1984), pp. 6-14.
Greelish, David A.
   "A Talk With the Creator?!
   -- An Interview with Ed Roberts."
   Historically Brewed (Issue #9, 1996), pp. 5-10.
Haas Mark.
   "The Texas Instruments Professional Computer."
   Byte (December 1983), pp. 286-324.
Harmon, Tom.
   "The SwTPC 6809 Microcomputer System."
   BYTE (January 1981), pp. 216-222.

Hauck, Lane T.
"System Description: The Noval 760."
Byte (September 1977), pp. 102-108.

Hudson, Richard L.
"French Entrepreneur Labors in Obscurity Despite His Big Feat:
Truong's Company Invented The First Microcomputer ..."
Wall Street Journal (September 18, 1985), pp. 1 & 27.

Infield, Glenn.
"A Computer in the Basement?"
Popular Mechanics (April 1968), pp. 77-229.
-- Author describes a home-built ECHO-IV computer.

Isaacson, Portia.
"Personal Computing: An Idea Whose Time Has Come."
Byte (February 1977), pp. 4 & 140-143.
-- Describes evolution of new trend in computing.

Johnson, Jeff., Teresa L. Roberts, William Verplank, David C.
Smith, Charles H. Irby, Marian Beard and Kevin Mackey.
"The Xerox Star: A Retrospective."
Computer (September 1989), pp. 11-29.

Jones, Douglas W.
"The DEC PDP-8 Story: The First Line of Truly
Small Computers."
Historically Brewed (Issues #7 to #9, 1994-1996).
Part I: The Beginning, (Issue #7, 1994), pp. 7-9.
Part II: The Minicomputer Revolution (Issue #8, 1995), pp. 7-10.
Part III: The Concluding Years, (Issue #9, 1996), pp. 11-14.

Kay, Alan and Adele Goldberg.
"Personal Dynamic Media."
Computer (March 1977), pp. 31-41.
-- Authors describe Dynabook, Alto and Smalltalk.

Kelly, Mahlon G.
"The Radio Shack TRS-80 Model 100."
BYTE (September 1983), pp. 139-162.

Krause, Llaus.
"Exidy Sorcerer."
The Analytical Engine (April - June 1994), pp. 22-23.

Layer, Harold A.
"Microcomputer History and Prehistory: An Archaeological Beginning."
Annals of the History of Computing, (Vol. 11, No 2, 1989), pp. 127-130.
Lemmons, Phil.
"Victor Victorious: The Victor 9000 Computer."
BYTE (November 1982), pp. 216-254.
Libes, Sol.
"The First Ten Years of Amateur Computing."
BYTE (July 1978), pp. 64-71.
Malloy, Rich.
"Little Big Computer: The TRS-80 Model 100 Portable Computer."
BYTE (May 1983), pp. 14-34.
McCallum, John C.
"The Sinclair Research ZX80."
BYTE (January 1981), pp. 94-102.
Miastkowski, Stan (Editor).
"Three New Computers from Radio Shack."
BYTE (October 1980), pp. 172-180.
Miller, Michael J.
"Looking Back: A history of the Technology that changed our world."
PC Magazine (March 25, 1997), pp. 108-136.
-- Part of *PC Magazine* Fifteen Years anniversary issue.
Mims, Forest M.
"The Altair Story."
Creative Computing (November 1984), pp. 17-27.
Morgan, Christopher P. (Editor-in-Chief).
"Hewlett-Packard's New Personal Computer: The HP-85."
BYTE (March 1980), pp. 60-66.
Nadeau, Michael E.
"The Littlest Zenith."
Byte (August 1989), pp. 94-96.
Perry, Tekla S. and Paul Wallich.
"Design case history: the Commodore 64."
IEEE Spectrum (March 1985), pp. 48-58.

Pfaffenberger, Bryan.
"The Social Meaning of the Personal Computer: Or, Why the Personal Computer Revolution was no Revolution."
Anthropological Quarterly (January 1988), pp. 39-47.

Poduska, Paul R.
"Building the Heath H8 Computer."
BYTE (March 1979), pp. 12-13 & 124-140.

Pournelle, Jerry.
"The Osborne Executive and Executive II: Adam Osborne's Improved Portable Computers."
BYTE (May 1983), pp. 38-44.

Press, Larry.
"Personal Computing: Where Did it Come From ?"
Abacus (Vol.1, No. 1, 1983), pp. 56-60.

Press, Larry.
"Before the Altair: The History of Personal Computing."
Communications of the ACM (Vol. 36, No. 9, September 1993), pp. 27-33.

Ramsey, David.
"Epson's HX-20 and Texas Instruments' CC-40."
BYTE (September 1983), pp. 193-206.

Roberts, H. Edward and William Yates.
"Altair 8800: The Most Powerful Minicomputer."
Popular Electronics (January 1975), pp. 33-38.

Ryan, Bob.
"Dynabook Revisited with Alan Kay."
BYTE (February 1991), pp. 203-208.

Scharf, Steve.
"LOBO MAX."
The Analytical Engine (April - June 1994), page 22.

Sheldon, Kenneth M.
"Micro Edsels: A look back at 15 years of the good, the bad, and marketing bombs of the microcomputer revolution."
Byte (February 1990), pp. 245-248.

Smith, David Canfield, Charles Irby, Ralph Kimball, Bill Verplank and Eric Harslem.
"Designing the Star User Interface."
BYTE (April 1982), pp. 242-282.

Thompson, Tom and Nick Baran.
"The NeXT Computer."
BYTE (November 1988), pp. 158-175.

Thompson, Tom and Ben Smith.
"Sizing Up the Cube: The long-awaited NeXT cube offers advanced features but only fair performance."
Byte (January 1990), pp. 169-176.

Tomayko, James E. (Editor).
"Electronic Computer for Home Operation (ECHO): The First Home Computer."
IEEE Annals of the History of Computing (Vol. 16, No. 3, 1994), pp. 59-61.

Toong, Hoo-min D. and Amar Gupta.
"Personal Computers."
Scientific American (December 1982), pp. 87-107.

Uttal, Bro.
"TI's Home Computer Can't Get in the Door."
Fortune (June 16, 1980), pp. 139-140.
-- Describes marketing problems of the TI-99/4 computer.

Uttal, Bro.
"A Computer Gadfly's Triumph,"
Fortune (March 8, 1982), pp. 74-76.
-- Describes Adam Osborne's introduction of the Osborne 1 portable computer.

Uttal, Bro.
"Sudden Shake-up in Home Computers."
Fortune (July 11, 1983), pp. 105-106.

Van Name, Mark L. and Bill Catchings.
"The Painlessly Portable PC."
Byte (August 1989), pp. 161-164.
-- Describes NEC UltraLite portable computer.

Wadlow, Thomas A.
"The Xerox Alto Computer."
BYTE (September 1981), pp. 58-68.

Warren, Jim.
"personal and hobby computing: an overview."
IEEE Computer (March 1977), pp. 10-22.

Williams, Gregg.
   "The Commodore VIC 20 Microcomputer: A Low-Cost,
   High-Performance Consumer Computer."
   BYTE (January 1981), pp. 94-102.
Williams, Gregg.
   "The Epson HX-20: The First Byte-sized Computer."
   BYTE (April 1982), pp. 104-106.
Williams, Greg.
   "The Epson QX-10/Valdocs System."
   BYTE (September 1982), pp. 54-57.
Wood, Lamont.
   "The Man Who Invented the PC."
   Invention & Technology (Vol. 10, No. 2, Fall 1994), page 64.
Worthy, Ford S.
   "Here Come the Go Anywhere Computers."
   Fortune (October 17, 1983), pp. 97-98.
   -- Describes TRS-80 Model 100 and other portable computers.

Apple Computer

Apple II and III:

Duprau, Jeanne and Molly Tyson.
   "The Making of the Apple IIGS."
   A+ Magazine (November 1986), pp. 57-74.
Edwards, John.
   "Apple IIe."
   Popular Computing (March 1983), pp. 108-190.
Helmers, Carl.
   "A Nybble on the Apple."
   Byte (April 1977), page 10.
   -- Editor of *Byte* previews Apple II computer.
Helmers, Carl.
   "An Apple to BYTE."
   BYTE (March 1978), pp. 18-46.
   -- An early review of the Apple II computer.
Little, Gary B.
   "A Close Look At Recent IIe Enhancements."
   A+ Magazine (August 1985), pp. 45-54.
Little, Gary, B.
   "A Technical Overview of the Apple IIGS."
   A+ Magazine (November 1986), pp. 45-52.
Markoff, John.
   "The Apple IIc Personal Computer."
   BYTE (May 1984) pp. 276-284.
Moore, Robin.
   "The Apple III and Its New Profile."
   BYTE (September 1982), pp. 92-132.
Moore, Robin.
   "Apple's Enhanced Computer, the Apple IIe."
   BYTE (February 1983), pp. 68-86.
Morgan, Christopher.
   "The Apple III."
   BYTE (July 1980), pp. 50-54.

Williams, Greg.
  "C is for Crunch,"
  BYTE (December 1984), pp. A75-A121.
  -- Author interviews Peter Quinn, who was design
  manager for the Apple IIe and IIc computers.
Williams, Greg and Richard Grehan.
  "The Apple IIGS."
  BYTE,(October 1986), pp. 84-98.
Wozniak, Stephen.
  "System Description: The Apple II."
  BYTE (May 1977), pp. 34-43.
  -- A technical description of the initial Apple II computer by the
  designer.

Lisa and Macintosh:

Craig, David T.
  "The Apple Lisa Computer: A Retrospective."
  The Analytical Engine (Vol. 2.1, July-September 1994),
  pp. 18-31.
  -- Contains an extensive list of references.
Lemmons, Phil.
  "An Interview: The Macintosh Design Team."
  BYTE (February 1984), pp. 58-80.
Markoff, John and Ezra Shapiro.
  "Macintosh's Other Designers."
  BYTE (August 1984), pp. 347-356.
  -- Includes interview with Jef Raskin.
Morgan, Chris, Greg Williams and Phil Lemmons.
  "An Interview with Wayne Rosing, Bruce Daniels and Larry
  Tesler: A behind-the-scenes look at the development of Apple's
  Lisa."
  BYTE (February 1983), pp. 90-114.
Nace, Ted.
  "The Macintosh Family Tree."
  Macworld (November 1984), pp. 134-141.

Nulty, Peter.
"Apple's Bid to Stay in the Big Time,"
Fortune (February 7, 1983), pp. 36-41.
-- Description of the technical and marketing strategies for Lisa computer.
Press, Larry.
"Apple Announces the Mac II and the Mac I 1/6."
Abacus (Vol. 4, No. 4, Summer 1987), pp. 58-62.
Raskin, Jef.
"The MAC and Me: 15 Years of Life with the Macintosh."
The Analytical Engine
Part 1: (Vol. 2.4, August 1995), pp. 9-22.
Part 2: (Vol. 3.3, May 1996), pp. 21-33.
Schlender, Brent.
"Steve Jobs Apple Gets Way Cooler."
Fortune (January 24, 2000), pp. 66-76.
Tesler, Larry.
"The Legacy of the Lisa."
Macworld (September 1985), pp. 17-22.
Van Nouhuys, Dirk.
"Apple 32 Past, Present, and Future."
A+ (July 1984), pp. 76-84.
Webster, Bruce F.
"The Macintosh."
BYTE (August 1984), pp. 238-251.
-- A system review of the Apple Macintosh computer.
Williams, Greg.
"The Lisa Computer System."
BYTE (February 1983), pp. 33-50.
Williams, Greg.
"The Apple Macintosh Computer."
BYTE (February 1984), pp. 30-54.
Williams, Greg.
"Apple Announces the Lisa 2."
BYTE (February 1984), pp. 84-85.
Webster, Bruce F.
"The Macintosh."
BYTE (August 1984), pp. 238-251.

Miscellaneous

A+ Magazine.
"Back In Time: Apple's ten-year history has been an eventful one.
here are some highlights."
A+ Magazine (February 1987), pp. 48-49.

Hogan, Thom.
"APPLE: The First Ten Years: History, Part I."
A+ Magazine (January 1987), pp. 43-46.
"APPLE: The First Ten Years: History, Part II."
A+ Magazine (February 1987), pp. 45-46.

Raleigh, Lisa.
"Woz on the Last 10 Years."
A+ Magazine (January 1987), pp. 39-41.

Schnatmeier, Vanessa.
"In Search of Early Apples."
A+ Magazine (August 1986), pp. A67-A70.

Williams, Greg. and Rob Moore.
"The Apple Story Part I: Early History."
BYTE (December 1984), pp. 67-71.
"The Apple Story Part II: More History and the Apple III."
BYTE (January 1985), pp. 167-174
-- informative interviews with Stephen Wozniak.

IBM

Alford, Roger C.
"The Fastest Portable: IBM's P75 Road Warrier."
BYTE (April 1991), pp. 265-268.
-- Reviews IBM PS/2 Model P75 portable computer.
Archer, Rowland.
"The IBM PC XT and DOS 2.00."
BYTE (November 1983), pp. 294-304.
Bond, George.
"The IBM PC Network."
BYTE (October 1984), page 111.
Bradley, David J.
"The Creation of the IBM PC."
BYTE (September 1990), pp. 414-420.
Curran, Lawrence J. and Richard S. Shuford.
"IBM's Estridge: The President of IBM's Entry Systems Division talks about Standards, the PC's simplicity, and a desire not to be different."
BYTE (November 1983), pp. 88-97.
Editors Bytes/Bits column (Byte, December 1975).
"Welcome IBM, to personal computing."
Reprint in *BYTE* (November 1983), page 137.
-- Reviews IBM 5100 portable computer.
Editors.
"Introduction: The Array of IBM Personal Computers."
BYTE (Fall 1984), pp. 9-26.
Fisher, Anne B.
"Winners (and Losers) from IBM's PC JR."
Fortune (November 28, 1983), pp. 44-48.
Gens, Frank and Chris Christiansen.
"Could 1,000,000 IBM Users Be Wrong?"
BYTE (November 1983), pp. 135-141.
Henry, G.G.
"IBM small-system architecture and design: Past, present and future."
IBM Systems Journal (Vol. 25, Nos. 3/4, 1986), pp. 321-333.
-- Provides details of the PC RT computer system.

Killen, Michael.
"IBM Forecast: Market Dominance."
BYTE (Fall 1984), pp. 31-38.
-- Reviews mainly the IBM 3270 PC and PC/XT Model 3270.
Lemmons, Phil.
"The IBM Personal Computer: First Impressions."
BYTE (October 1981), pp. 27-34.
Littman, Jonathan.
"The First Portable Computer."
PC World (October 1983), pp. 294-300.
-- Describes IBM SCAMP computer.
Malloy, Rich.
"Two New Office Products from IBM."
BYTE (December 1983), page 594.
-- Reviews IBM 3270 PC and PC/XT 370.
Malloy, Rich.
"IBM Announces the PCjr,"
BYTE (December 1983), page 358.
Malloy, Rich., G. Michael Vose and Tom Cluwe.
"The IBM PC AT."
BYTE (October 1984), pp. 108-111.
Mitchell, Robert.
"IBM and AT&T Enter the Fray of 386SX Notebook Computers."
BYTE (August 1991), pp. 252-254.
-- Describes IBM's first battery operated laptop computer and
competing product from AT&T.
Morgan, Chris.
"IBM's "Secret" Computer: The 9000."
BYTE (January 1983), pp. 100-106.
Reinhardt, Andy and Ben Smith.
"Sizzling RISC Systems from IBM."
BYTE (April 1990), pp. 124-128.
-- Describes RISC System/6000 workstations.
Sandler, Corey.
" IBM: Colossus of Armonk."
Creative Computing (November 1984), pp. 298-302.

Williams, Gregg.
   "A Closer Look at the IBM Personal Computer."
   BYTE (January 1982), pp. 36-68.
Vose, Michael G. and Richard S. Shuford.
   "A Closer Look at the IBM PCjr."
   BYTE (March 1984), pp. 320-332.

Software

Application programs

Cmar, Karen A.
  "AppleWorks: An Integrated Office Product."
  BYTE (December 1984), pp. A18-A22.
Lemmons, Phil.
  "A Guided Tour of Visi On."
  BYTE (June 1983), pp. 256-278.
Licklider, Tracy Robnett.
  "Ten Years of Rows and Columns: From a 16K-byte VisiCalc to
    multimegabyte packages, spreadsheets have come a long way in a
    decade."
  Byte (December 1989), pp. 324-331.
Ramsdell, Robert E.
  "The Flexibility of VisiPlot."
  BYTE (February 1982), pp. 32-36.

Languages

Bowles, Kenneth.
  "UCSD PASCAL: A Nearly Machine Independent Software
    System."
  BYTE (May 1978), pp. 46 & 170-173.
Editor
  "Design of Tiny BASIC."
  Dr. Dobb's Journal (Vol. 1, No. 1, January 1976).
Gates, Bill.
  "The 25th Birthday of BASIC."
  BYTE (October 1989), pp. 268-276.
Kay, Alan C.
  "The Early History of Smalltalk."
  ACM SIGPLAN Notices (March 1993), page 87.
Lehman, John A.
  "PL/I for Microcomputers."
  BYTE (May 1982), pp. 246-250.

Lockwood, Russ.
   "The Genealogy of BASIC."
   Creative Computing (November 1984), pp. 86-87.
Moore, Charles H.
   "The Evolution of FORTH, an Unusual Language."
   BYTE (August 1980), pp. 76-90
Rosner, Richard.
   "A Review of Tom Pitman's Tiny BASIC."
   BYTE (April 1977), pp. 34-38.
Tesler, Larry.
   "The Smalltalk Environment."
   BYTE (August 1981), pp. 90-147.
Woteki, Thomas H. and Paul A. Sand.
   "Four Implementations of Pascal."
   BYTE (March 1982), pp. 316-353.
Wozniak, Stephen.
   "SWEET16: The 6502 Dream Machine."
   BYTE (November 1977), pp. 150-159.

Operating Systems and User Interfaces

Hayes, Frank and Nick Baran.
   "A Guide to GUI's: Graphical user interfaces make computers
   easy to use; keeping them all straight is the hard part."
   BYTE (July 1989), pp. 250-257.
Hayes, Frank.
   "From TTY to VUI: As computers become more complex, using
   them becomes easier and easier."
   BYTE (April 1990), pp. 205-211.
   -- Describes development of graphic user interfaces.
Kildall, Gary.
   "CP/M: A Family of 8 and 16-Bit Operating Systems."
   BYTE (June 1981), pp. 216-232.
McHugh, Josh.
   "For the love of hacking."
   Forbes (August 10, 1998), pp. 94-100.
   -- Describes free-software and Linux operating system.

Perry, Tekla S. and John Voelcker.
"Of mice and menus: designing the user-friendly interface."
IEEE Spectrum (September 1989), pp. 46-51.

Graphics Software

Bissell, Don.
"The Father of Computer Graphics: Today's graphics systems
owe their existence to an innovative graduate school project
called Sketchpad."
BYTE (June 1990), pp. 380-381.
Editor.
"The CAD Revolution: A 20-Year Saga."
Compressed Air Magazine (October/November 1993), pp. 40-44.
Sutherland, Ivan E.
Sketchpad: A Man-Machine Graphical Communication System."
*AFIPS Conference Proceedings (Vol. 23), 1963 Spring Joint
Computer Conference*, pp. 329-346.
Sutherland, Ivan E.
"Computer Graphics."
Datamation (May 1966), pp. 22-27.

Microsoft

Brant, Richard with Julia Flynn and Amy Cortese.
"Microsoft Hits the Gas: Its Bidding to Lead the Info Highway
Pack."
Business Week (March 21, 1994), pp. 34-35.

Isaacson, Walter.
"In Search of the Real Bill Gates."
Time (13 January, 1997), pp. 30-42.

Paterson, Tim.
"An Inside Look at MS-DOS: The design decisions behind the
popular operating system."
BYTE (June 1983), pp. 230-252.

Schlender, Brent.
"Bill Gates & Paul Allen Talk."
Fortune (October 2, 1995), pp. 68-86.

Simonyi, Charles and Martin Heller.
"The Hungarian Revolution."
BYTE (August 1991), pp. 131-138.

Stein, Joel.
"Image is Everything: Bill Gates bid for a digital empire may pay
off someday, but for now the King of Content can only scheme."
Time (11 November 1996), pp. TD32-TD38.
-- Describes Corbis company founded by Bill Gates.

Udell, Jon.
"Three's the One: Windows 3.0 carries DOS into the 1990's."
BYTE (June 1990), pp. 122-128.

Udell, Jon.
"Windows 3.1 Is Ready to Roll."
BYTE (April 1992), pp. 34-36.

Uttal, Bro.
"Inside the Deal that made Bill Gates $350,000,000,"
Fortune (July 21, 1986), pp. 23-33.

Companies, Organizations and People

Davidson, Clive.
"The Man who made Computers Personal."
New Scientist (June 19, 1993), pp. 32-35.
-- A biographical article on Alan Kay.
Fraker, Susan.
"How DEC Got Decked."
Fortune (December 12, 1983), pp. 83-92.
-- Describes DEC bureaucratic and marketing problems with its
  early personal computers.
Grover, Mary Beth.
"The Seagate Saga."
Forbes (May 4, 1998), pp. 158-159.
Halfhill, Tom R.
"R.I.P. Commodore 1954 - 1994."
BYTE (August 1994), page 252.
Hof, Robert D.
"The Sad Saga of Silicon Graphics: What went wrong at the
  company that once made everybody say: "Gee Whiz."
Business Week (August 4, 1997), pp. 66-72.
Jacob, Rahul.
"The Resurrection of Michael Dell."
Fortune (September 18, 1995), pp. 117-128.
Kirkpatrick, David.
"Over the Horizon with Paul Allen."
Fortune (July 11, 1994), pp. 68-75.
Kraar, Louis.
"Acer's Edge: PCs To Go."
Fortune (October 30, 1995), pp. 186-204.
Lesser, Hartley.
"Exec Avant-Garde: The Dynamic Zone."
Softalk (November 1983), pp. 66-70.
Petre, Peter D.
"Mass-Marketing the Computer."
Fortune (October 31, 1983), pp. 60-67.

Petre, Peter.
"The Man Who Keeps the Bloom on Lotus: Mitch Kapor, a child of the Sixties, has nurtured Lotus Development Corp into the world's largest independent software company."
Fortune (June 10, 1985), pp. 136-146.

Ramo, Joshua Cooper.
"How AOL Lost the Battles but Won the War."
Time (September 22, 1997), pp. 42-48.

Ramo, Joshua Cooper.
"Andrew S. Grove: A Survivor's Tale."
Time (December 29, 1997 - January 5, 1998), pp. 30-46.
-- This was a special "Man of the Year" issue featuring Andrew Grove.

Schlender, Brent.
"The Adventures of Scott McNealy: Javaman Pow!"
Fortune (October 13, 1997), pp. 70-78.

Serwer, Andy.
"Michael Dell Rocks."
Fortune (May 11, 1998), pp. 58-70.

Tazelaar, Jane Morrill (Editor).
"BYTE, 15th. anniversary SUMMIT: 63 of the world's Most Influential People in Personal Computing Predict the Future, Analyze the Present."
BYTE (September 1990), pp. 218-366.
-- Provides a short biographical background of the participants.

Uston, Ken.
"Behind The Scenes At Brøderbund: A Family Affair."
Creative Computing (September 1984), pp. 157-162.

Uttal, Bro.
"Xerox Xooms Toward the Office of the Future."
Fortune (May 18, 1981), pp. 44-52.

Uttal, Bro.
"The Man Who Markets Silicon Valley."
Fortune (December 13, 1982), pp. 133-144.
-- Describes success of Regis McKenna and his company.

Uttal, Bro.
"Sudden Shake-up in Home Computers."
Fortune (July 11, 1983), pp. 105-106.

Uttal, Bro.
"The Lab That Ran away From Xerox."
Fortune (September 5, 1983), pp. 97-102.
-- Describes Xerox's failure to market the results of research at its Palo Alto Research Center (PARC).

Weiss, Eric A.
"The Computer Museum."
Abacus (Vol. 2, No. 4, Summer 1985), pp. 60-65.

Whitmore, Sam.
"Electronic Arts."
Cider (May 1984), pp. 35-37.

Wolfe, Tom.
"The Tinkerings of Robert Noyce: How the sun rose on the Silicon Valley."
Esquire (December 1983), pp. 346-374.
-- An informative biographical article on Robert Noyce

Wright, Robert.
"The Man Who Invented the Web: Tim Berners-Lee started a revolution, but it didn't go exactly as planned."
Time (May 19, 1997), pp. 44-48.
-- describes development of the World Wide Web

Yuln, Matt.
"Exec Electronic Arts: Software Construction Company."
Softalk (August 1984), pp. 36-40.

Miscellaneous

Ahl, David H. (Editor, In-Chief)
   "Tenth Anniversary Issue of Creative Computing."
   Creative Computing (November 1984), Vol. 10, No 11.
Anderson, John L.
   "Dave Tells Ahl: The History of Creative Computing."
   Creative Computing (November 1984), pp. 66-77.
Bouchard, Judith W. (Editor-in-Chief).
   Micro Computer Abstracts (Formerly *Micro Computer Index*).
   -- A quarterly journal of microcomputing abstracts.
Buchholz, W.
   "The Word "Byte" comes of Age..."
   BYTE, (February 1977), page 144.
Caulkins, David.
   "A Computer Hobbyist Club Survey."
   BYTE (January 1977), pp. 116-118.
Editors.
   "Clubs and Newsletters Directory."
   BYTE (October 1979), page 210.
Friedrich, Otto.
   "Machine of the Year."
   Time (January 3, 1983), pp. 12-24.
Helmers, Carl.
   "The Era of Off-the-Shelve Personal Computers Has Arrived."
   BYTE (January 1980), pp. 6-98.
Nelson, Ted.
   "On the Xanadu Project."
   BYTE (September 1990), pp. 298-299.
Press, Larry.
   "Is There Such a Thing as a Personal Computer."
   Abacus (Vol. 1, No. 2, Winter 1984), pp. 69-71.
Press, Larry.
   "The ACM Conference on the History of Personal Workstations."
   Abacus (Vol. 4, No. 1, Fall 1986), pp. 65-70.
Shapiro, Fred R.
   "The First Bug."
   BYTE (April 1994), page 308.

The Staff of inCider/A+.
   "100 issues of inCider: A Look Back."
   inCider/A+ (April 1991), pp. 36-39.
Tomayko, James E. (Editor).
   "Origin of the Term Bit."
   "Origin of Word Byte and The First Bug."
   Annals of the History of Computing,
      (Volume 10, Number 4, 1989), pp. 336-340.

Microprocessors

Antonoff, Michael.
"Gilbert Who?: An obscure inventor's patent may rewrite microprocessor history."
Popular Science (February 1991), pp. 70-73.
Baskett, Forest and John L. Hennessy.
"Microprocessors: From Desktops to Supercomputers."
Science (Vol. 261: 13 August 1993), pp. 864-871.
Bylinsky, Gene.
"The Second Computer Revolution."
Fortune (February 11, 1980), pp. 230-236.
-- Details impact of microprocessor.
Bylinsky, Gene.
"Intel's Biggest Shrinking Job Yet."
Fortune (May 3, 1982), pp. 250-256.
-- Describes development of 432 microprocessor.
BYTE Staff.
"Micro, Micro: Who Made The Micro ?"
BYTE (January 1991), pp. 305-312.
Diefendorff, Keith.
"History of the *PowerPC Architecture*."
Communications of the ACM (June 1994), pp. 28-33.
Editors.
"The Microprocessor at 25: Milestones of a Quarter Century."
PC Magazine (December 17, 1996), pp. 147-149.
Faggin, Federico.
"The Birth of the Microprocessor."
BYTE (March 1992), pp. 145-150.
Frenzel, Lou
"How to Choose a Microprocessor."
BYTE (July 1978), pp. 124-139.
-- Reviews microprocessors and applicable microcomputers.
Garetz, Mark.
"Evolution of the Microprocessor."
BYTE (September 1985), pp. 209-215.

Gwennap, Linley.
"Birth of a Chip: In only 25 Years, the microprocessor has become the life-support system of the modern world."
BYTE (December 1996), pp. 77-82.

Halsema, A.I.
"A Preview of the Motorola 6800."
BYTE (April 1979), pp. 170-174.

Mazor, Stanley.
"Microprocessor and Microcomputer: Invention and Evolution."
The Analytical Engine (Vol. 3.4, Fall 1996), pp. 6-13.

Moore, Charles R. and Russell C. Stanphill.
"The PowerPC Alliance."
Communications of the ACM (June 1994), pp. 25-27.

Moore, Gordon E.
"Cramming More Components Onto Integrated Circuits."
Electronics (Vol. 38, no.8), April 19, 1965, pp. 114-117.

Moore, Gordon E.
"Intel: Memories and the Microprocessor."
Daedalus (Vol. 125: No 2, 1996), pp. 55-80.

Morse, Stephen P., William B. Pohlman, & Bruce W. Ravenel.
"The Intel 8086 Microprocessor: A 16-bit Evolution of the 8080."
IEEE Computer (June 1978), pp. 18-27.

Morse, Stephen P., Bruce W. Ravenel, Stanley Mazor and William B. Pohlman.
"Intel Microprocessors: 8008 to 8086."
IEEE Computer (October 1980), pp. 42-60.

Noyce, Robert N. and Marcian E. Hoff.
"A History of Microprocessor Development at Intel."
IEEE Micro (February 1981), pp. 8-21.

Rampil, Ira.
"Preview of the Z-8000."
BYTE (March 1979), pp. 80-91.

Ritter, Terry and Joel Boney.
"A Microprocessor for the Revolution: The 6809."
BYTE (January 1979), pp. 14-42.

Schlender, Brent.
   "Killer chip."
   Fortune (November 10, 1997), pp. 70-80.
   -- reviews the Intel Merced microprocessor.

Hardware and Peripherals

Christensen, Clayton M.
"The Rigid Disk Drive Industry: A History of Commercial and Technological Turbulence."
Business History Review (Winter 1993), pp. 531-588.

Gaskin, Robert R.
"Paper, Magnets and Light: The long history of data storage devices is intertwined with the more recent, meteoric rise of personal computers."
BYTE(November 1989), pp. 391-399.

Jarrett, Thomas.
"The New Microfloppy Standards."
BYTE (September 1983), pp. 166-176.

Lancaster, Don.
"TV Typewriter."
Radio-Electronics (September 1973), pp. 43-50.

Lebow, Max.
"Tele-Vic: Commodore Breaks the $100 Price Barrier for Modems."
BYTE (March 1982), pp. 240-246.

Lemmons, Phil.
"A Short History of the Keyboard."
BYTE (November 1982), pp. 386-387.

Levy, Steven.
"Of Mice and Men: The Mouse is but a small part of Doug Engelbart's larger quest."
Popular Computing (May 1984), pp. 70, 75-78.

Mayadas, A.F., R.C. Durbeck, W.D. Hinsberg and J.M. McCrossin.
"The evolution of printers and displays."
IBM Systems Journal (Vol. 25, Nos. 3/4,1986), pp. 399-416.

Mendelson, Edward.
"Microsoft Does a Wheelie: With a wheel between its buttons, the IntelliMouse goes where no other mouse has gone before."
PC Magazine (17 December 1996), page 65.

Morgan, Chris.
"A Look at Shugart's New Fixed Disk Drive."
BYTE (June 1978), pp. 174-176.

Nulty, Peter.
"Big Memories for Little Computers."
Fortune (February 8, 1982), pp. 50-56.
-- Describes development of hard disk drives by Seagate and
Shugart.
Pang, Alex and Soojung-Kim.
"The Making of the Mouse: Apple Computer is commonly
credited with having simply popularized someone else's idea – but
it wasn't really like that at all."
Invention & Technology, (Winter 2002, Volume 17, Number 3),
pp. 48-54.
Pelczarski, Mark.
"Microsoft SoftCard."
BYTE (November 1981), pp. 152-162.
Peters, Chris.
"The Microsoft Mouse."
BYTE (July 1983), pp. 130-138.
Schnatmeier, Vanessa.
"A Modern Mouse Story."
A+ (July 1984), pp. 32-35.
Scientific American.
"The Solid-state Century: the past present and future of the
transistor."
Scientific American (Special issue, January 1998).
-- Includes articles on integrated circuit and microprocessor
technology.
Whang, Min-Hur and Joe Kua.
"Join the EISA Evolution: The EISA bus is breaking up that old
"Gang of Nine"."
Byte (May 1990), pp. 241-247.
Wieselman, Irving L. and Erwin Tomash.
"Marks on Paper: Part 1 and Part 2. A Historical Survey of
Computer Output Printing."
Annals of the History of Computing,
-- Part 1: Volume 13, Number 1, 1991.
-- Part 2: Volume 13, Number 2, 1991, pp. 203-222.

Historical Timelines

Ahl, David H.
   "Ascent of the Personal Computer."
   Creative Computing (November 1984), pp. 80-82.
BYTE Staff.
   "10 Years of BYTE: Special anniversary Supplement."
   BYTE (September 1985), pp. 198-208.
Halfhill, Tom R.
   "Apple's Technology Milestones."
   B*YTE* (December 1994), pp. 52-60.
Smarte, Gene and Andrew Reinhardt.
   "1975-1990: 15 Years of Bits, Bytes and Other Great
   Moments."
   B*YTE* (September 1990), pp. 369-400.
Williams, Gregg and Mark Welch.
   "A Microcomputer Timeline."
   BYTE (September 1985), pp. 197-208.

Early Computer Technology

Randell, Brian.
  "The Origins of Computer Programming."
  IEEE Annals of the History of Computing (Vol. 16, No.4, 1994),
  pp. 6-14.
Reid-Green, Keith S.
  "A Short History of Computing."
  BYTE (July 1978), pp. 84-94.
Ridenour, Louis N.
  "Computer Memories."
  Scientific American (Vol. 192, No.6, June 1955)
  -- An overview of computer memory technology in the mid
  1950's.
Stern, Nancy.
  "Who Invented the First Electronic Digital Computer?"
  Abacus (Vol. 1, No. 1, 1983), pp. 7-15.

Part Three ...

What Was The First Personal Computer?

By: Roy A. Allan.

Defining Terms

Recent literature is inconsistent in defining "the first personal computer" as the term is presently understood. This has resulted, to an extent, from limited awareness of some early products with a claim to the title. Which computer was truly the first to be personal in the modern sense?

This article does not discuss the early personal use of mainframe computers; it also excludes experimental computers, such as the MIT Memory Test Computer, and minicomputers, because they were not oriented to the consumer market. In an article entitled "Is There Such a Thing as a Personal Computer?" [7], Lawrence I. Press presented several criteria – such as architecture, software, physical characteristics and marketing – which would serve to distinguish a personal computer.

Thus, for the purposes of this article, the term "personal computer" requires clarification. Up to the mid-1970's, when the majority of computers were mainframes shared by many users, a "personal" computer was defined as being designed for use by one person. As the technology progressed, our understanding of the term has changed; we now consider some early hardware too large and too expensive to qualify as being "personal," and require that "a PC" should also be small, easy to use, and of relatively low cost. Today's personal computer has evolved into a desktop appliance, available through the consumer market, that provides ready and affordable computing power to an individual. In this context, which of the early computers then called "personal" should we consider for the distinction of being "the First"?

1957: The IBM Auto-Point

John L. Lentz at IBM developed a small Personal Automatic Calculator (PAC) in the late 1940's, and described an engineering model of PAC in December 1954. This project evolved into the IBM 610 computer, described by the reference work "IBM's Early Computers" [1] as being "IBM's first Personal Computer." The Model 610, also called the Auto-Point, was announced in September 1957, with a purchase price of $55,000. The computer system consisted of a floor-standing cabinet – incorporating the electronics, magnetic drum, plug-board, and separate paper-tape readers and punches – with a keyboard for input and an electric typewriter for output. It was not a stored-program computer; a programmer entered instructions from the keyboard, or input them through the paper-tape readers.

Scientists and engineers used the Auto-Point computer to solve small scientific and engineering problems. IBM built about 180 units, but was not then an aggressive competitor in the development of small computer systems. Other organizations such as Bendix Aviation, Librascope, Digital Equipment Corporation (DEC) and the Massachusetts Institute of Technology (MIT), were thus able to participate in an emerging market and developed, respectively, the G-15, LGP-30, PDP Series and LINC small computer systems.

1963: MIT LINC

Gordon Bell, a principal in the design of early DEC PDP-Series minicomputers, has stated that the MIT LINC was the first personal computer. MIT developed LINC – an acronym for "Laboratory INstrument Computer" – to facilitate the use of computer technology in biomedical research laboratories [3]. Principal designers were Wesley Clark and Charles Molnar. MIT demonstrated a prototype in early 1962 and completed sixteen units by mid-1963, which were assembled by scientific users to improve their understanding of the system. LINC had four console modules, an electronics cabinet and keyboard. The processor logic circuits used transistorized circuit modules from DEC. An oscilloscope module could display a 512-by-512-point image. Memory was magnetic core with a basic capacity of 1,024 twelve-bit words; two magnetic-tape drives provided additional storage. Each system cost about $32,000. Initial software was a text editor, an assembler and some utilities. A small number of scientific laboratories used the LINC computer in dedicated applications.

The IBM 610 and the MIT LINC were "personal" computers developed with reference to established larger architectures, at a cost which confined their use to major scientific organizations. In the late 1960's a company called Computer Terminal Corporation (CTC) took the opposite tack by starting development of a "smart" computer terminal which would incorporate a microprocessor.

1971: Datapoint 2200
An Invention & Technology article [11] quotes Jack Frassanito as saying "I invented the personal computer..." CTC hired Frassanito in 1969 to develop a computer terminal that would have its own processor and other circuitry which would allow it to mimic other major computer manufacturers' terminals. The self-contained unit included a 12-line display, keyboard, two cassette tapes, a Texas Instruments bit-serial processor supported by TTL logic, 8K bytes of internal memory. CTC introduced the resulting Datapoint 2200 in June 1970, and shipped the first units in early 1971.

Although CTC designed the unit purely as a terminal with unprecedented capabilities, a number of commercial users wrote programs and used it as an early, small, desktop computer. The Datapoint 2200, however, was still not made available at a price attractive to an individual user. The first personal computer with a price affordable to an individual user in a potentially larger market was the Kenbak-1.

1971: Kenbak-1
An Early Model Personal Computer Contest, sponsored by the Computer Museum of Boston, ComputerLand and CW Communications in 1986, selected the Kenbak-1 as being the first personal computer. The criterion for selection of the winner was "interest, significance and date of each model" [5]. Designed by John V. Blankenbaker and introduced in late 1971, the computer used 130 small and medium-scale integrated circuits and had a memory of 256

8-bit bytes; it processed 1000 instructions per second. Input and output were very limited, with no keyboard or screen. Blankenbaker sold only 40 units at a price of $750 [4].

The Kenbak-1, with its primitive user interface, stands in sharp contrast to history's next "first personal computer" – the stunningly innovative, feature-rich and costly Alto, developed by the Xerox Palo Alto Research Center (PARC) in California.

1973: Xerox Alto

According to Alexander and Smith's "Fumbling the Future: How Xerox Invented, Then Ignored, the First Personal Computer" [9], Xerox developed the Alto computer as a research project in the early 1970's; construction of the prototype was begun in November 1972 and completed in April 1973. Lead engineers included Chuck Thacker, Larry Tesler, Butler Lampson, Peter Deutsch, Bob Metcalfe and several others. Intended sale price of a system was about $30,000, and the production cost of early examples was nearly that high. An Alto computer system consisted of a main tower case intended to fit under a desk, cabled to a grayscale bit-mapped display screen, 8 inches horizontal by 10 inches vertical, that could display 60 lines of 90 characters – a full portrait page. Input was by keyboard supplemented by the "mouse" originally designed by Douglas Engelbart at SRI. The processor was a 16-bit custom made unit and basic memory was 64K 16-bit words, expandable to 256K. One or two 2.5 megabyte pack-type hard-disk drives were installed in the main cabinet. PARC also developed a new interactive programming language called Smalltalk which was used to create a windowed graphic environment and the desktop metaphor that was an unprecedented synthesis of hardware and software. Furthermore, PARC surrounded its individual Altos with a resource pool that included an Ethernet network, shared laser printers, and electronic mail. These were new human interface concepts that eventually formed the basis for developments by Apple Computer, Microsoft and others.

But the Alto, like computers previously described, and like contemporary systems including the National Radio Institute NRI 832 kit, Hewlett-Packard HP 9830A programmable calculator, EPD

System One computer kit and IBM 5100 portable computer, still relied on discrete components. Use of discrete logic kept production labor-intensive and limited the designer's ability to achieve a low system price. Technological developments at Intel Corporation were about to surmount this last obstacle to the affordable small computer.

1971: Intel

Intel introduced large-scale integrated memory chips and microprocessors in the early 1970's, providing the basis for low-cost personal microcomputers. The company released the 4-bit, 4004-based SIM-4 simulator board – the first commercial product incorporating a microprocessor – in May 1972, followed by the 8008-based SIM-8. The Intellec 4 and Intellec 8 development systems, or "blue boxes," followed in August 1973 [6].

The SIM-4 was not a computer, but a design aid to facilitate the development of microprocessor applications. Implementation of the microprocessor in commercial computing really started with the European Micral.

1973: Micral

The French Micral microcomputer developed by REE (Recherches et Études Életroniques) was the earliest personal computer to use a microprocessor [2 & 5]. Truong Trong Thi managed the company and released the computer, which sold for $1,950, in January 1973. The unit included an Intel 8008 microprocessor and 256 bytes of RAM, expandable to one kilobyte.

France had produced the first microcomputer. Another year would go by before the first North American microcomputer was advertised in the March 1974 issue of *QST*, an amateur radio magazine.

1974-5: Early US Microcomputers

The first personal computer in the USA to use a microprocessor was the Scelbi-8H, designed by Nat Wadsworth and Robert Findley of Scelbi Computer Consulting, Inc. in Milford, CT. Described in advertisements as "The totally new and very first – Mini-computer," the 8H used the Intel 8008 microprocessor and up to 4K bytes of memory. In kit form it sold for "as low as $440." The price was right, but Wadsworth had health problems, and a change in the company's first priority – to publishing – resulted in poor sales of the computer.

The first "magazine project" microcomputer, called the Mark-8, was designed by Jonathan A. Titus and appeared In the July 1974 issue of *Radio-Electronics* [10]. It used the Intel 8008 microprocessor and had 256 bytes of memory. Enthusiasts could buy plans from the magazine for a nominal amount, or a substantially complete kit of parts for $350; sales were insignificant. Today, just over twenty years later, a Mark-8 is one of the most valuable and sought-after of all historical micros.

It was a misfortune of both the Scelbi-8H and the Mark-8 to stumble and fall in the darkness just before dawn. Only a few months later, a New Mexico-based company called MITS – Micro Instrumentation and Telemetry Systems – could not cope with the orders it received when it introduced the Altair microcomputer.

1975: Altair 8800

The January issue of *Popular Electronics* [8] featured the Altair 8800 developed by Ed Roberts of MITS – although the unit on the magazine's cover was only a painted, empty case. It used the Intel 8080 microprocessor, and basic memory was only 256 bytes. A 100-pin bus with 16 slots facilitated expansion of the system with additional memory and peripherals. Kit price by mail order was $397. The Altair 880 was a startling success, and a flood of orders created severe delivery problems at MITS; in theory, the same computer was available assembled and tested for $621, but customers who ordered a finished unit waited for months while the factory caught up.

In retrospect, the Altair's position in the vanguard of the microprocessor revolution is puzzling. The layout of the hundred-pin Altair bus (more commonly known today as the "S-100 bus") was deeply compromised and made the design of third-party peripherals unnecessarily difficult. MITS' own add-on products were sometimes poorly engineered, like the 4K dynamic memory boards, or sometimes were announced but never produced. And if the hardware was attractively priced, the software was not; a paper tape of Bill Gates and Paul Allen's "Micro-soft" Altair BASIC interpreter sold for $150.

Regardless, the combination of the Altair hardware and the Microsoft BASIC interpreter was the first runaway success of the "personal computer" industry. More sophisticated products with better promotion, like the Apple II computer introduced in June 1977 and IBM's PC released in August 1981, gave substantial computing power to the consumer in the mass market. Which of these early computers we can honor as "the First" will depend on our narrow and literal, or broad and inclusive, interpretation of the term "personal computer" – which has obviously meant many things to many people over the past forty years!

Conclusion

The IBM 610 Auto-Point Computer was the earliest personal computer, but it did not use the stored–program concept. The MIT LINC used the stored-program concept, but was a limited scientific project with no impact in the general market. The Kenbak-1, the first low-cost personal computer, had a very limited interface and enjoyed few sales. Xerox' Alto introduced many of the concepts widely used in computers today, but was a "personal computer" only in a rarefied environment and at prohibitive cost. The French REE Micral was the first personal microcomputer to use a microprocessor. The Scelbi-8H and the Mark-8 were the first US microcomputers, but did not have a significant success in the market. The Altair 8800 – with a more powerful microprocessor, an innovative BASIC interpreter and an affordable price – was "the first" personal computer to be a commercial success and start a "personal" technological revolution.

Bibliography

1. Bashe, Charles J., Johnson, Lyle R., Palmer, John H. and
   Pugh, Emerson W.
   IBM's Early Computers."
   Cambridge: MIT Press, 1986, pp 505-508.
   -- Describes the Personal Automatic Calculator (PAC) and the
   IBM 610 Auto-Point Computer.

2. Buchholz, Werner (Editor).
   "Was the First Microcomputer Built in France?"
   Annals of the History of Computing.
   Vol. 10, No. 2, 1988, p. 142.
   -- Describes the Micral microcomputer.

3. Clark, W. A. and Molnar, C. E.
   "A Description of LINC."
   Stacy, Ralph W. and Waxman, Bruce W. (Editors).
   Computers in Biomedical Research.
   New York: Academic Press, 1965, pp 35-66.

4. Editor.
   "Early Small Computers."
   Annals of the History of Computing.
   Vol. 11, No. 1, 1989, pp. 53-54.
   -- Discusses the IBM 610, Kenbak-1 and Micral computers.

5. Juliussen, Egil and Isaacson, Portia.
   "Computer Industry Almanac."
   Dallas, Texas: Computer Industry Almanac, Inc., 1987,
   pp. 288-289.
   -- Briefly describes the Kenbak, Micral and Altair computers.

6. Noyce, Robert N. and Hoff, Marcian E.
   "A History of Microprocessor Development at Intel."
   IEEE MICRO, February 1981, pp. 8-21.
   -- Describes the SIM-4 & 8 and Intellec 4 & 8 development
   boards.

7. Press, Larry.
   "Is There Such a Thing as a Personal Computer."
   Abacus, Vol. 1, No. 2, Winter 1984, pp. 69-71.
   -- Describes "What really distinguishes personal computers from
      mainframes?"

8. Roberts, H. Edward and Yates, William.
   "Altair 8800... The Most Powerful Minicomputer."
   Popular Electronics, January 1975, pp. 33-38.

9. Smith, Douglas K. and Alexander, Robert C.
   "Fumbling The Future: How Xerox Invented Then Ignored, The
   First Personal Computer."
   New York: William Morrow and Co., Inc., 1988.
   -- Describes development of the Alto computer.

10. Titus, Jonathan A.
    "Computer! – Build This Minicomputer Yourself."
    Radio-Electronics, July 1974, pp. 29-33.
    -- Describes the Mark-8 microcomputer.

11. Wood, Lamont.
    "The Man Who Invented the PC."
    American Heritage of Invention & Technology,
    Vol. 10, No. 2, Fall 1994, p. 64.
    -- Describes the Datapoint 2200 "smart" terminal.

World of Wishes
Pony Wishes

Carol Barton

Illustrated by Charlotte Alder

SCHOLASTIC

First p̶ʳⁱⁿᵗᵉᵈ ⁱⁿ ᵗʰᵉ　　　　　　　　　　　　　　　Books

Registere̶d　　　　　　　　　　　　　　　　　　747 0RA
SCHOL̶ASTIC ᵃⁿᵈ　　　　　　　　　　　　　　　gistered

Text copyright © Carol Barton, 2007
Illustrations © Charlotte Alder, 2007

The right of Carol Barton to be identified as the author of this work
and the right of Charlotte Alder to be identified as the illustrator of this
work has been asserted by them.

10 digit ISBN 1407 10334 2
13 digit ISBN 978 1407 10334 1

British Library Cataloguing-in-Publication Data
A CIP catalogue record for this book
is available from the British Library

Typeset by M Rules
Printed in the UK by CPI Bookmarque, Croydon, CR0 4TD
Papers used by Scholastic Children's Books are
made from wood grown in sustainable forests.

1 3 5 7 9 10 8 6 4 2

This is a work of fiction. Names, characters, places, incidents
and dialogues are products of the author's imagination or are
used fictitiously. Any resemblance to actual people, living or
dead, events or locales is entirely coincidental.

www.scholastic.co.uk/zone

Contents

For Daniel, with love

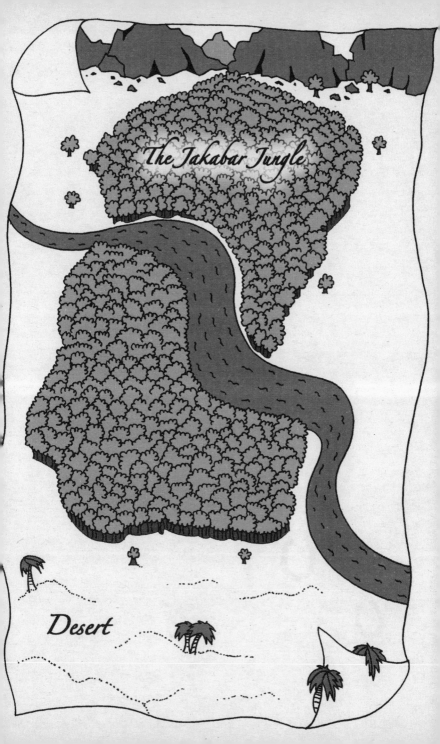

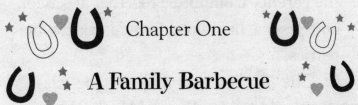

Chapter One

A Family Barbecue

"Maddie, take these salads outside, please. Dad's nearly ready to start barbecuing and the guests will be arriving soon."

"All right." Maddie sighed and picked up two bowls of salad from the kitchen table.

"You *are* looking forward to this, aren't you?" Her mother looked up anxiously from where she was putting the finishing touches to a mouth-watering array of puddings.

"Yes . . . I suppose so," Maddie replied. "I just wish the Coatsworths weren't coming."

"Maddie, we've been through all this," said her mother with a sigh. "We had to ask them. We've been to two barbecues at their home, Mrs Coatsworth and I are on the Parents' Committee together at school, and Jessica has often invited you to her parties."

"She invites everyone in the class," protested Maddie. "It would look odd if she left me out. But she doesn't like me, Mum."

"Well, I'm sorry, but I'm afraid you're just going to have to make the best of it. And I still think that if you are friendly towards Jessica sooner or later maybe she'll start being friendly to you."

"Maybe. . ." said Maddie dubiously.

"She *did* ask you if you wanted to go horse riding with her. . ."

"Only so that she can show off because

2

she knows I can't ride," Maddie replied. "Now I don't have the brace on my teeth any more she wants to find something else she can tease me about."

"Well, you could always have some riding lessons," said her mother as she piped cream on to a large dish of fresh strawberries.

Maddie shook her head. "I don't think so." She turned and went out into the back garden. Her father, wearing a blue and white striped apron over his shorts, had just started to barbecue a large selection of steaks, burgers and sausages. He waved a pair of tongs at Maddie as she placed the bowls of salad on a long trestle table that had been set up on the lawn. She waved back, then wandered away under the rose-covered trellis and down the garden. She knew what her mother had said about the Coatsworth family was right, but she still wished they weren't coming. She'd tried

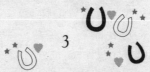

really hard to be friends with Jessica but Jessica still continued to make horrible remarks about her and Maddie knew she'd only asked her to go horse riding so that she could laugh at Maddie when she fell off.

The friends she would really have liked to invite to the barbecue (apart from her best friend Lucy and her family, who were also coming) were her friends from the magical land of Zavania but she knew that was impossible. It had been some time since she'd seen Sebastian and Zak the raven, Zenith the WishMaster and his housekeeper Thirza, and she hoped that the only reason they hadn't come to fetch her was because no one had a wish to be granted.

It was early evening and the shadows were lengthening in the garden as the sun sank in the west. Snatches of music from the sound system that her father had set up

4

drifted through the trees, and as the sun set Maddie knew that the many fairy lights they had concealed amongst the shrubs would start to glow.

She was about to turn and walk back to the patio to see if her mother wanted any more help but, perhaps because Sebastian and the others had been on her mind, she suddenly felt an urge to check to see if their boat was there under the willows. Hardly a day went by that she didn't look and usually she was disappointed, but today she had a strong feeling that, just maybe, they might be there.

It was cool and silent under the willows with barely a ripple on the water and certainly no boat to be seen. Maddie stood on the bank for a while, but when the sound of voices reached her from the top of the garden, suggesting that the first of the guests had started to arrive, she turned to go.

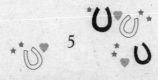

5

It was then that a movement in the corner of her eye caught her attention. At once she stopped and peered through the branches of the willow tree until, to her delighted and utter amazement, she saw a boat edge its way through the willows. Zak the raven was perched as always at the front, while Sebastian stood in his usual place at the back, guiding the boat into position with a long pole.

They seemed almost as surprised to see her as she was to see them. "Well, bless my soul!" said Zak at last. "She's already here waiting for us, Sebastian."

"Maddie!" Sebastian exclaimed. "You must have guessed we were coming."

"Saves me going to find her," muttered Zak.

"Oh," cried Maddie. "I didn't know you were coming. How could I? I just hoped you might. I come down here nearly every day, in case you might be here."

"Do you?" said Sebastian in amazement.

"Yes," Maddie mumbled, suddenly embarrassed at what she had just revealed. "At least, I do when I have the time," she added, trying to sound casual.

"Yeah, right," said Zak, and she knew that she hadn't deceived the wily old bird for one moment.

"Has someone made a wish?" she asked in an attempt to change the subject.

"Well, that's the general idea," said Zak. "We're not out on a picnic, you know!"

"Shut up, Zak," said Sebastian. As the raven tossed his head and turned his back on him, he brought the boat skilfully alongside the bank of the stream. Looking at Maddie again, he said, "Yes, Maddie, someone has made a wish and once again I would like your help with the spells."

"Oh yes," said Maddie, "of course I'll help . . . the only thing is. . ." She turned and looked up the garden uncertainly.

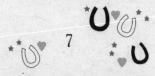

"What's wrong?" asked Sebastian.

"We are having a barbecue," Maddie explained. "Lots of people are coming and I . . . I'll have to be there." She paused and looked from Sebastian to Zak and then back to Sebastian again. "I don't suppose," she said slowly, "I don't suppose you two would like to come. . .?" When they both remained silent, she went on. "You see, all our friends have been invited. We've even invited Jessica Coatsworth and you know I don't really like her . . . while you two, well, you are two of the best friends I've ever had . . . and I just thought. . ."

"Ah, Maddie," said Sebastian sadly, "it's a nice idea, but you know it isn't possible. Zenith only allows us into your world to collect you; he would never allow us to do any more."

Maddie looked anxiously over her shoulder. "The trouble is, people have started to arrive and I have to go and help."

"We'll have you back in no time at all," Sebastian promised.

And they would, Maddie knew that. In past assignments, it seemed that from the moment she first stepped aboard Sebastian's boat until the moment she stepped back on to the bank, time had stood still.

After only another moment's hesitation Maddie held out her hand. "All right," she said. Sebastian grasped her hand and helped her aboard the boat, where she sat down among the brightly coloured cushions. Sebastian immediately eased his boat away from the bank and through the overhanging willow branches.

"I need your help, Maddie," he said. "Zenith is leaving shortly to go on a visit with the king and queen and he's entrusted me with this particular wish. I don't want anything to go wrong."

"Which it well might if you're left to

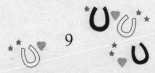

9

your own devices," sniggered Zak from his vantage point at the front of the boat. They'd left the shelter of the willows now and were moving swiftly downstream to the faster flowing river. The countryside was already changing; the fields were a more vibrant green, the sky a deeper blue and the flowers more brightly coloured than any Maddie had seen in her own world.

"So who has made this wish," asked Maddie, ignoring the raven's remark, "and what is it for?"

"It's a pony," said Sebastian. "His name is Gus and he's part of a group of ponies who are visiting the summer school in Zavania for flying lessons."

"Do you mean winged ponies?" cried Maddie. When Sebastian nodded she clasped her hands together. "How lovely!"

"Yes," Sebastian agreed, "but there is one big problem for Gus."

"And what is that?" Maddie leaned forward attentively.

"His wings haven't grown."

"So is that his wish?" Maddie's eyes widened.

"You've got it in one," chortled Zak.

"It shouldn't be too difficult," Sebastian went on. "We'll go straight to the East Tower, choose the ring for the conductor of magic, write the spells, then take ourselves off to the ponies' summer school."

"Trouble is," said Zak, "whenever we think something isn't going to be too difficult it turns out to be a real nightmare."

"To tell you the truth," said Sebastian, ignoring Zak's comments, "it's been pretty chaotic in Zavania for the last few days."

"Oh?" said Maddie. "And why is that?"

"We've had a visitor," Sebastian replied, and Zak gave a muffled snort as if he hadn't been too impressed by this particular guest.

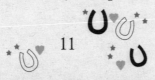

11

"His name is Zoltan and he is a – an old wizard friend of Zenith's – apparently they were at magic school together."

"So why has it been chaotic?" asked Maddie.

"Well, it hasn't been just Zoltan," Sebastian explained. "He brought a whole entourage with him and they seem to have caused havoc amongst the castle staff with their constant demands and complaining. We've actually had the wizard himself and his two bodyguards staying at the East Tower and Thirza is almost at her wits' end."

"Oh dear," said Maddie, "poor Thirza, I know how she feels – like I said, we've had to invite Jessica Coatsworth to our barbecue."

"Her again," muttered Zak. "Why are you inviting *her*?"

"Mum says we have to," Maddie replied. "I think she thinks that if we are nice to

12

her she'll be nice in return – but I can't see that happening."

"Hummp!" Zak growled in agreement.

"And you say that Zenith is off on a royal visit?" asked Maddie.

"Just for a day or so," Sebastian replied, "but Thirza has had to prepare for that as well – I think she'll be glad to see the back of them all."

"Sounds as if this could be an interesting trip," said Maddie, leaning back against the cushions and trailing her hand in the water.

"Yes," he agreed, "even though the actual wish doesn't sound too complicated."

"Tell me about these flying ponies," said Maddie after a moment. "Where do they live, Sebastian?"

"They don't really have a fixed home; they fly from place to place. But their parents all send them to the flying school for their lessons, then after that they join

13

up with their herd ready to migrate to the south. Gus came along with the others in the hopes that his wings would grow but nothing has happened – he still just has a couple of little bumps on his back where his wings should be."

"Poor little pony," said Maddie. "Let's hope we can help him."

By this time they were moving rapidly through a steep-sided gorge and very soon Maddie could see the turrets and the pennants fluttering on the royal castle. As always she felt a little stab of excitement on approaching Zavania.

They moored the boat at the castle jetty, but as they were making their way through the beautiful gardens the peace was disturbed by all sorts of commotion.

"Hello," said Zak, cocking his head on one side. "What's happening now?"

"Sounds like Zoltan and his party are just leaving," said Sebastian.

"Well, that's a relief," muttered the raven.

As they rounded the corner they saw that a party of people were loading baggage on to horse-drawn carriages. "That's Zoltan over there," said Sebastian, nodding towards a tall, imposing figure with flowing black hair who was dressed entirely in red: a red tunic and scarlet trousers and a long crimson cloak. "And those are his two bodyguards – Boris and Wulfric."

"I don't like the look of them," whispered Maddie. One was short and squat with a huge stomach and bandy legs – rather like Harromin, the fat toad who lurked in the gorge. The other was taller, bald and with huge muscular arms.

"You should try having them stay with you," muttered Zak.

"No thanks," said Maddie with a little shiver.

Zenith and Thirza stood on the steps of

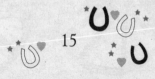

the East Tower, watching as their guests boarded the carriages. Zenith was just as Maddie remembered him; in his long black robes and single gold earring, he stood with his legs apart and arms folded. Finally, and with much shouting, the rest of Zoltan's entourage lined up, the carriages started to move and within moments all that was visible was a huge cloud of dust kicked up by the horses' hooves and the carriage wheels.

With a sigh Zenith turned and caught sight of the friends. "Oh, there you are," he said, and Maddie got the impression he wasn't in the best of moods. "I have to leave immediately, so you will be on your own, but you at least know what you have to do."

"Of course, Zenith," Sebastian replied.

"You shouldn't have any problems," said Zenith as he took the bag that Thirza passed to him. "It's all perfectly straightforward and as far as I can see there's nothing that can go wrong."

"Now, where have I heard that before?" chuckled Zak as they watched Zenith make his way up to the main entrance of the royal castle.

Chapter Two

The Spells

"So did Zenith leave any further instructions for us?" asked Sebastian as the friends followed Thirza into the East Tower.

"He said to tell you that you can choose which ring you want to use as your conductor of magic," Thirza replied in her high-pitched voice, "but that you have to base your spells around the letter J."

"No problem," said Maddie. "I always

think the letter J is quite a fun letter – jester and jokes, words like that."

"Well, take yourselves up to the turret room and get to work," said Thirza. "And you, Zak –" She turned to the raven. "You needn't think you can go off somewhere for a crafty snooze! No, you can come and help me clear up the mess Zoltan's lot left behind."

"Eh, what?" Zak looked indignant, but even he didn't dare argue with Thirza in the mood she was in.

Maddie followed Sebastian up the steep spiral staircase to Zenith's turret room.

"Well," Sebastian said, looking around at the shelves of bottles and jars filled with pills and potions of every colour imaginable, "we'd best get started. We'll choose the ring first." Crossing to the display cabinet that Maddie knew housed the collection of precious rings used as

19

conductors of magic, he unlocked the glass lid and lifted it back.

As Maddie walked towards the case, a shaft of sunlight pierced one of the tiny panes of glass in the window of the turret room and caused a blinding flash from one of the stones. "Ooh, Sebastian," she breathed, "just look at that stone, it's almost as if it was telling us to choose it."

"Very well," said Sebastian, "I trust your judgement, Maddie – the sapphire it shall be." Leaning forward, he lifted the ring from its bed of black velvet and slipped it on to his finger. "Now," he said as he closed the lid and locked the case, "we have to write the spells."

They made their way together into Zenith's library. It was here, surrounded by stacks of the WishMaster's dusty old books on magic, that they began the important job of constructing the spells.

It took much longer than they had

expected, and this time even Maddie found it something of a battle to find the exact words they needed to make the spells. By the time they had finished the sun was setting and they were both tired and hungry.

"About time!" squawked Zak when they finally emerged from the turret room. "I thought you'd dozed off."

"The writing of the spells is much more difficult than you realize," muttered Sebastian.

"Humph! We'd better get a move on if we're to get over to the summer school before dark," grumbled Zak.

"No one's going anywhere," said Thirza firmly. "It's much too late. You will all have supper and a good night's sleep, then first thing in the morning you can take yourselves off to grant your wish."

"Sounds like a good idea to me," sighed Zak in relief.

"But—" Sebastian began.

That was as far as he got, however, for Thirza intervened again. "I can't send you out in the dark with no food inside you, so no more arguments – a few hours more aren't going to make any difference to when that pony grows his wings."

Thirza served the friends a delicious supper, after which she escorted Maddie to a small room in the tower where she was to spend the night. She was asleep almost before her head touched the pillow.

Maddie awoke to bright sunlight that flooded into the room and spilled across her bed. For a moment she couldn't think where she was, then, with a sudden rush of excitement she remembered. Thinking of the task that lay ahead of them, she pushed back the patchwork quilt that had kept her so warm and cosy throughout the night and stepped out on to the cold stone floor.

When she went downstairs it was to

find that Sebastian and Zak were already at the table while Thirza served them breakfast of warm, crusty bread spread with golden butter.

"Oh, you are up at last," said Zak as he pecked at his bread.

"I'm sorry if I'm late," said Maddie, "my bed was so cosy. . ."

"You're not late, Maddie," said Sebastian. "Take no notice of Zak."

"That's right," sighed Zak. "Take no notice of me – no one ever does."

After breakfast they took their leave of Thirza. "We shouldn't be too long," said Sebastian. "We only have to go and see Gus and grant his wish. It shouldn't take long at all – in fact I doubt we even need two spells – but Zenith has always insisted we have two."

"Quite right," said Thirza, "you never know what you might encounter, even between here and the summer school!"

23

"Where is the summer school exactly?" asked Maddie after they'd left the East Tower.

"It's in the castle grounds – in the far corner of the paddocks behind the royal mews," Sebastian replied.

After they'd gained access to the castle they made their way across the courtyard, beneath a stone archway and into the mews where all the king's animals were housed. But that was as far as they got, for the rows of stalls were in uproar. Grooms were running to and fro, horses were whinnying in fear and in the middle of all the mayhem stood the Princess Lyra, her long golden hair dishevelled and her clothes awry as she shouted and stamped her foot in anger.

"Oh my giddy aunt!" squawked Zak. "Whatever is going on here?"

"Looks like trouble," muttered Sebastian, while Maddie's heart sank in

24

despair. Anything involving the spoilt Princess Lyra usually spelt trouble.

Suddenly the princess caught sight of Sebastian and she stopped her shouting and stamping. "Ah," she cried, "Sebastian! Just the person. I demand you use one of those spells of yours to help me."

"Your Royal Highness." Sebastian gave a little bow. "Whatever is wrong?"

"Wrong?" she cried, casting wild glances around her as the poor grooms scuttled away to a place of safety. "I'll tell you what is wrong. Three of my best ponies have been stolen. That is what is wrong!"

"Stolen?" Sebastian frowned. "But whoever would steal royal ponies? No one in Zavania, that's for sure."

"I don't know who it is," spluttered the princess, her voice rising again, "but when I catch them they will be sorry. I will make them pay dearly for their cheek, but at the moment all I'm concerned with is getting

25

the ponies back. I have a horse show coming up soon and I intend riding all three ponies in different events."

"Well, I'm very sorry about this," said Sebastian, "but I don't see how I can help . . . you see—"

"Of course you can help!" The princess gave him no chance to explain further. "Like I said, you can use one of your spells to have my ponies returned to me."

"Oh boy!" muttered Zak, and hid his head under his wing.

"But that is just what I *can't* do," said Sebastian patiently. "You see, I have already set out on an assignment to grant another wish, and my spells are to be used for that."

"So what is this other wish?" demanded the princess. At that moment she seemed to become aware of Maddie. "And what's *she* doing here again?"

"Maddie helps me with granting the

26

wishes," said Sebastian quietly. "I couldn't manage without her." At his words Maddie felt herself blush. "As for the wish we are granting," he went on, "it has been made by one of the ponies at the summer school for flying ponies."

"So what does this pony want?" demanded the princess, with a scathing glance in Zak's direction. In the past she had made more than one dire threat against the raven who, no doubt mindful of this, immediately hid his head again.

"His wings haven't grown," Sebastian explained. "His wish is for his wings to grow so that he can fly away and join the rest of his herd before their migration south. I can't just leave an assignment once it has begun. If I did, we would all have to contend with Zenith's anger."

The thought of that seemed to subdue the princess, though only a little. She scowled for a moment, then suddenly

looked up again, her eyes narrowing. "When you grant one of these wishes," she said, "you have two spells, don't you?"

"Here we go," muttered Zak.

"Yes," Sebastian agreed, "that's perfectly true, because we usually need two spells."

"I know all that," said the princess impatiently, "but I can't see you'll need two spells for this wish. The summer school is only across the paddocks, for goodness' sake! There's not a lot can happen in the time it will take you to get there."

"Can you do that, Sebastian?" asked Maddie anxiously. "Can you grant two wishes with one set of spells?"

"I don't know," Sebastian admitted, "I've never had to do it before."

"Well, I *demand* you do it this time," said the princess, tossing her head in the air. "If you don't, you will have my father, the king, to answer to on his return."

"I suppose we could try," said Sebastian

dubiously, "but I'm not at all sure it will work and we must grant Gus's wish first."

"In that case I'm coming with you," declared the princess.

"Oh great," muttered Zak, "that's all we need!"

Together with the princess, the friends left the royal mews and set off across the meadow to the far paddock, home to the famous flying school. The sight that met their eyes there almost took Maddie's breath away. There were several small ponies in the field, all pure white, and each with a pair of beautiful rainbow-coloured wings. An elderly man appeared from the stable block and began to instruct the ponies. "That's Rupert," murmured Sebastian. "He trains the ponies to fly." As the friends watched, the ponies began to trot around the edge of the paddock, then broke into a canter before taking off into the wind, their manes and tails streaming

out behind them as they circled overhead before coming in to land once more.

"Oh!" cried Maddie in delight. "I've never seen anything like it; they are so beautiful!"

"Hello there," called Sebastian as the old man walked towards them. "We've come to see Gus about granting his wish."

"Well. . ." Rupert pushed back the cloth cap he wore and scratched his head. Maddie thought the old man looked wary when he saw that the Princess Lyra was with them. "I know you said you were coming and Gus was getting really excited about it – that's why what's happened doesn't make sense."

"What do you mean?" said Maddie gently.

"Well, he's gone," said Rupert.

"What do you mean, he's gone?" demanded the princess, her eyes narrowing.

"What I say, Your Highness," Rupert replied. "He was here yesterday but when I went to his stall this morning with his feed there was no sign of him."

31

Chapter Three

Edgar

"So where on earth could he be?" cried Maddie.

"I wonder if this could be the same thing that has happened to your ponies, Your Highness," said Sebastian.

"Oh, I doubt it," the princess replied haughtily. "My ponies are highly-trained thoroughbreds – hardly the same thing as a winged pony."

"But no one would have known he was

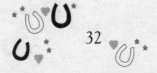

a winged pony," said Maddie, "because he doesn't have his wings yet. He would have just looked the same as any other pony."

"That's true," Sebastian agreed, "assuming that the ponies have all been stolen."

"What else could have happened to them?" demanded the princess.

"Maybe they just got fed up and decided to go off on a jolly," Zak remarked.

"My ponies had everything they could have wished for," declared the princess, "so what on earth could they have got fed up with?"

"What indeed?" Zak said slyly, and shrugged his wings.

"Z. . .a. . .k," said Sebastian warningly. Turning to the others, he said, "I think we have to assume that the ponies and Gus have been stolen. What we need to do now is to find out who has taken them."

"Where were your ponies stolen from?"

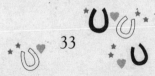

asked Maddie, glancing at the princess.

The princess looked down her nose. "Who asked you to interfere?"

"Right," said Sebastian firmly, "let's get one thing straight. If I'm to attempt to help you, Your Royal Highness, then it goes without question that Maddie and Zak are to be fully involved, is that understood?"

As Maddie and Zak held their breath, the princess pulled a face and then sniffed in agreement.

"So," Sebastian went on, "in answer to Maddie's question, where did your ponies disappear from?"

"They were in their paddock yesterday but when their grooms went to fetch them this morning they weren't there." The princess paused. Narrowing her eyes, she said, "Can't you use a spell or something to find them?"

"I can't use spells at the drop of a hat!"

"Well, let's face it," said the princess

with a shrug, "you can't grant your pony's wish if he isn't here, can you?"

"No," Sebastian agreed, "that is why our first task is to find Gus; and maybe if we find Gus then we might find your ponies at the same time."

"If the ponies were stolen, someone must have seen something," said Maddie thoughtfully.

"Yes, but who?" The princess spread her hands impatiently. "I've already questioned all the grooms and stable boys and no one saw anything."

"There is someone who sees everything that goes on in Zavania," said Zak suddenly.

"Are you thinking what I'm thinking?" Sebastian turned to the raven.

"Yep." Zak nodded. "I think we need to pay a visit to Edgar."

"Who is Edgar?" asked Maddie, looking from one to the other.

"You'll see!" said Zak.

35

"He lives on a plateau – high above Zavania," Sebastian explained. "But he really does keep an eye on everything that goes on. You're right, Zak, we need to pay him a visit. We can travel most of the distance in the boat but we would need to climb the rocks up to the plateau. It's quite a rough climb – are you up for that, Maddie?"

"Oh yes, of course," said Maddie.

"I'm coming too," said the princess.

Maddie's heart sank, Zak drew in his breath sharply and Sebastian opened his mouth to protest but the princess held up her hand. "Don't bother," she said sharply. "I'm coming and that's that."

With Zak muttering under his breath they took their leave of Rupert and made their way back through the royal mews to the jetty. It wasn't the first time the princess had travelled with them on the boat and Maddie could not help but notice

how she took the best seat amongst the cushions, leaving only a very small space for Maddie herself.

They took a short journey downstream towards a large rocky outcrop that loomed ahead, and it seemed in no time at all Sebastian was securing the boat to a gorse bush, steadying it with one foot while the two girls alighted on to a narrow rocky pathway.

The path was not only narrow and rocky it was also incredibly steep and in a very short time everyone, with the exception of Zak, who flew beside them, was huffing and puffing.

"Oh for goodness' sake," gasped the princess, "how much further?"

"We're nearly there," said Sebastian. They stumbled on for a short way, scrambling between gorse bushes, until quite suddenly the pathway came to an end and a large, flat, open space stretched

before them.

"This is it," said Sebastian, "the Eyrie Plateau." He paused. "Now, I wonder where Edgar is. . ."

They all looked around but there didn't seem to be anyone else on the plateau.

"There's no one here," gasped Maddie. "Have we climbed all up here for nothing?"

And then, quite suddenly, everything seemed to grow dark as a large shape blotted out the light from the sun and a strange whirring sound filled the air.

"Oh," cried Maddie, "what is happening?" She looked up and there, hovering above them, was the largest bird she had ever seen. Its wingspan was huge, its beak curved and wicked-looking while its cruel, outstretched talons looked as if they meant business. "Sebastian!" she cried. "It's going to attack us. Do something, quickly!" The huge bird came in to land only a few yards away. "We'll

have to use a spell. . ." Maddie went on desperately, as the bird turned its head and glared at them. "There's nothing else that can help us up here. . ."

"For goodness' sake," said Zak, and to her

amazement Maddie realized that the raven, instead of being terrified as she would have expected, appeared to be laughing. Even the princess looked bored and faintly contemptuous. "It's only Edgar!"

"Edgar?" said Maddie, still eyeing the huge bird uncertainly.

It was Sebastian who explained. "Edgar is an eagle, Maddie. I'm sorry – we should have explained."

"Yes," said Maddie rather huffily, "I think you should have! He nearly frightened me to death." She took a deep breath. "So he isn't going to attack us then?"

"No, of course not," said Zak. "First-rate fellow is Edgar. In actual fact, he's a distant relative of mine. Only by marriage, of course ... my cousin's sister-in-law married—"

"Yes, all right, Zak," Sebastian interrupted, "we don't have time for that now. If you really want to be helpful you can go over and ask Edgar if he's willing to talk to us."

"Fine," said Zak, and flounced off across the plateau towards the eagle, who

continued to watch them all with a beady eye.

"I don't know why you bother with that stupid raven," snapped the princess. "He's such a pain."

"No, he isn't," said Maddie, springing to Zak's defence, "and if I remember rightly, you didn't think he was a pain when he was helping to rescue your brother."

The princess fell silent after that and a few moments later Zak hopped back.

"Well," asked Sebastian, "what did he say?"

"I had to tell him why we were here before he would agree to talk to us," said Zak.

"For pity's sake!" The princess almost exploded. "Doesn't he know who I am?"

"Oh yes," Zak replied dryly, "he knows only too well, but it didn't make much difference."

"So what did he say?" asked Sebastian

quickly, before the princess could explode again.

"Ah, now, *there* we have a story – and what a story it is." Zak puffed out his chest feathers. "He said he sees everything up here," he went on, "and that, yes, he did see both Gus and the princess's ponies being taken away."

"Did he say who took them?" demanded the princess.

"I think you'd better come over and hear this for yourselves," said Zak and Maddie noticed that he sounded rather uneasy.

"Greetings, Edgar," Sebastian hailed the eagle who nodded his head in response. "We understand that you saw the ponies being taken away. Can you tell us, please, who took them?"

"There were two men," said Edgar in a gruff voice.

"Do you know who they were?"

demanded the princess impatiently.

"They were not of Zavania," Edgar replied.

"Then who. . .?" Sebastian began.

"I was flying over Zavania yesterday before sunset," Edgar replied. "I saw these men leading the little pony who doesn't yet have his wings – at first I didn't think too much about it but then they coaxed him into a covered wagon. I hung around for a while just to see what was happening, then I saw them go into the adjoining paddock and round up three more ponies and lead them away too."

"My ponies!" screeched the princess and everyone jumped in fright. "Why didn't you stop them or tell someone, you silly creature?"

Edgar turned his head, glared at the princess, then flapped his great wings.

"Oh boy!" muttered Zak.

"I didn't realize the ponies were in

danger," the eagle said coldly.

"No, quite," said Sebastian hastily. "No one's suggesting you could have done anything—"

"I am!" declared the princess. "Those ponies are valuable and my father the king will be none too pleased to find them gone when he gets back."

"In that case," said Edgar in the same cool tone, "you'd better go and get them back again."

"Those men. . ." said Maddie, turning to Edgar. "Can you describe them?"

"Yes," the eagle replied, "one was short and squat and the other big and burly."

"Oh dear," said Maddie. "Are you thinking what I'm thinking, Sebastian?"

"Yes," Sebastian relied grimly, "I'm afraid I am, they sound like the wizard's bodyguards, don't they? I wonder if Zoltan himself knew about the theft of the ponies. . ."

"Isn't Zoltan a friend of Zenith's?" said Maddie.

"He is." Sebastian sounded worried. "And with Zenith away, I can't consult him. . ."

"What is there to consult about?" cried the princess. "My ponies have been stolen – it looks like we know who has taken them. I demand you get them back."

"I'm not sure it's that easy," said Sebastian uncomfortably.

"Don't forget, Sebastian," said Maddie, "that they have Gus as well, and we have Gus's wish to grant, which means we would have to find him anyway."

"Yes, I know." He still sounded uneasy. "But I don't like Zoltan's involvement in all this. What if it all goes horribly wrong?"

"Zenith wouldn't like the idea of those ponies being stolen," said Zak suddenly, "no matter who it was who had taken

45

them. I think we should go and find them, right now."

"That's the most sensible thing I've ever heard you say," said the princess, staring at Zak.

"OK," said Sebastian slowly, "but first we'd need to find out where Zoltan lives. I suppose Thirza might know. . ."

"I know where Zoltan the Wizard is," Edgar put in. "He used to live in the desert, but for some reason he's recently moved to a wild mountainous area to the east of the Jakabar Jungle."

"So how would we get there?" asked Maddie.

"Use one of your spells," said the princess flippantly.

"There might not be any need for that," said Edgar, flapping his great wings again and making them all jump. "I have a friend who has just started an air service that travels from here on the plateau to the

Jakabar Jungle and back. You might be able to persuade him to take you all."

Maddie looked up into the sky, wondering if she could see this aircraft that Edgar was talking about, but the sky was clear and blue without so much as a cloud, let alone a plane. "When will your friend be here?" she asked.

"Be here?" said Edgar. "He's here already. He arrived last night and he's due to take off again this morning."

"But where is he?" Maddie looked around in bewilderment.

"Over there." Edgar nodded towards a gorse bush on the far side of the plateau. The bush wasn't very big and was gnarled and twisted and bent almost double by the fierce winds that blew on the high flat ground.

Maddie frowned and shielded her eyes from the sun. It didn't seem possible that this small bush could conceal *anything*, let alone an aircraft.

47

"Come on," said Edgar. "I'll take you over and introduce you to Tariq; he's resting after his journey."

"Is Tariq the pilot?" asked Maddie as they all began to follow Edgar across the flat expanse of ground.

"Pilot?" repeated Edgar with a frown. "Well, yes, I suppose you could say that."

They cautiously approached the bush as Edgar strutted round behind it, and as they peered into its short spiky branches, Maddie stared in amazement. All she could see was a tiny figure curled up asleep on a long roll of what looked like canvas. As they stared, Edgar nudged the little figure with his beak and it stirred, stretched, and sat up, rubbing its eyes.

"Well, my giddy aunt!" exclaimed Zak. "It's a monkey!"

Chapter Four

Morning Flight to Jakabar

The figure was indeed that of a monkey, dressed in a pair of green trousers, a tiny red waistcoat and a little black hat trimmed with sequins and a tassel.

"Wake up!" said Edgar. "Looks like you have yourself some passengers."

The monkey scrambled to its feet and stood with hands on hips, surveying the friends suspiciously. "Who are you?" he said at last.

49

Sebastian stepped forward. "I'm Sebastian, Junior WishMaster," he said, "and this is Her Royal Highness the Princess Lyra of Zavania, my friend Maddie, and Zak, the raven."

"Will he be coming with us?" asked the monkey, looking Zak up and down.

"Of course he will," said Sebastian, as Zak began to puff out his chest in indignation. "Do you have a problem with that?"

"Not as long as he doesn't try to interfere with the flying arrangements," said the monkey. "We always seem to have trouble when we try to transport anything with wings."

"I'm sure there won't be any trouble," said Sebastian, frowning warningly at Zak, who looked as if he might be about to explode.

"Let's hope not," said the monkey. "My name is Tariq," he continued, still keeping

a wary eye on Zak. "The flight to Jakabar will be taking off shortly."

"Er, excuse me," said Maddie, stepping forward, "but what exactly are the flying arrangements?"

"What do you mean?" the monkey snapped.

"Well, what are we actually flying in?"

"It's more like what we are flying *on*," he replied briskly. Jumping off the roll of canvas, he bent down, took the edge in his tiny hands, and with a flick of his wrists unrolled it.

Maddie gasped in astonishment, for instead of the dull old piece of canvas as she had imagined, it turned out to be the most beautiful of carpets with an intricate pattern depicting exotic birds and flowers worked in the finest materials in glowing, jewel-like colours.

"Welcome aboard the morning flight to Jakabar," said the monkey, leaping on to

51

the carpet and dancing about. "I trust your journey will be a pleasant one."

"You mean we've got to travel on *that*?" squawked Zak. "Well, you can forget it. No way. I shall fly myself."

"I said he'd be trouble," snapped the monkey.

"Zak," said Sebastian sternly. "I think that just for once you need to do as you are told."

"You're joking!" Zak almost exploded. "This may be OK for you guys, but you haven't got any choice. I'm perfectly capable of flying myself."

"Maybe he has a point," said Maddie, sensing a battle.

"He'd never make it," sneered Tariq. "He'd drop from exhaustion, probably over the desert, and you'd never hear from him again."

"Then maybe we should just let him," said the princess unkindly.

52

"Right," said Sebastian, "that's enough! I'm going to pull rank here. *I'm* in charge of this assignment. Zak, you will travel with the rest of us and like it. I don't want any more argument. The matter is closed. And there are two other points we need to clear up." He turned to the princess. "Do you intend travelling with us, Your Royal Highness?"

"Of course I do," said the princess haughtily and Maddie's heart sank.

"In that case we need to let the castle know where you are, otherwise there will be a search party out looking for you."

"The pigeons will be up here later on for any post," said Edgar, "I'll tell them."

"You'd better tell them to tell my brother the Crown Prince Frederic," put in the princess, "because our parents are away."

"You said there were two points," said Maddie, with a glance at Sebastian.

"Yes," he agreed. Turning to the princess again, he went on, "Your Royal Highness, for the duration of this assignment I would like your permission for us all to call you Lyra. As you know from previous experience, it's not always a good idea to advertise the fact that we have royalty with us."

The princess didn't reply immediately and Maddie thought she was going to refuse. Then she tossed her head and shrugged. "I suppose so," she said at last, "just as long as you revert back to my title when we return to Zavania and that during this assignment you never, for one moment, forget who I am."

"Fat chance of that," muttered Zak.

"OK. So we all know the ground rules," said Sebastian. "Let's go."

"Right," said the monkey, "now that's all settled, we'll start boarding. This way, please."

Maddie stepped on to the carpet, followed by Lyra. They moved forward until they were right in the centre. It was a large carpet, larger than it had first appeared, and at each end it had a row of knotted tassels.

"Sit down!" commanded Tariq bossily. Turning to Zak, who had his back to them and hadn't boarded, he said, "Move along there, please. Quick sharp!"

"All right!" muttered Zak. He strutted angrily forward, then flounced aboard the carpet without so much as a glance at the monkey, who had taken up his position at one end and was sitting cross-legged ready for take-off.

"Goodbye!" Edgar called. "See you when you get back."

The monkey began chanting a curious little song in his high-pitched voice, while Maddie felt the carpet beneath her begin to wrinkle.

"Sebastian. . ." she whispered. She clutched his arm, then, as she felt the carpet begin to move and lift up from the ground, she could bear it no longer and squeezed her eyes tightly shut. The wind caught her curls and tossed them around her head, while in her ears all she could hear was a strange rushing sound. After that, all was silent, an awesome silence, and then her ears popped.

"Maddie, Maddie, you must look! It's incredible, fantastic. . ." Sebastian was tugging at her arm and at last she forced herself to open her eyes. For a moment she felt overwhelmingly dizzy and a little bit sick as she realized just how high they were in the sky. Taking a deep breath, she forced herself to look down.

Far, far below she could see Zavania, the tops of the trees and the river like a silver snake as it wound its way through the gorge. She could even see the royal castle with the flags fluttering from the turrets. "Oh," she cried in excited amazement, "if Thirza came outside we could wave to her! Oh Sebastian, isn't it absolutely wonderful!"

"I can't see what all the fuss is about." Zak gave a loud sniff. "I do this every day of the week."

Maddie realized that the princess was being unusually quiet, and when she turned and looked at her she saw that the other girl had her eyes tightly shut and that she had turned a rather peculiar colour.

"Oh dear," said Maddie, reaching out her hand and lightly touching her arm, "are you all right, er, Lyra?"

"Leave me alone," mumbled the princess.

"But. . ."

"I said, leave me alone!"

"All right." Maddie shrugged and turned away.

"Look, Maddie!" Sebastian clutched her arm again. "There's the Enchanted Forest – you can see how big it is from up here."

Maddie gave a little shiver as she looked down at the dense darkness of the forest and remembered the times their adventures had taken them into its depths.

"What's the matter with Lyra?" murmured Sebastian a little later, noticing that the princess still had her eyes tightly shut.

"I don't think she likes flying," Maddie whispered. "I think it's making her feel ill. She said she wants to be left alone."

They fell silent after that, content to watch as the magic carpet flew away from Zavania and veered away to the south, until – with the endless blue of the sky

above them – they began to pass over a flat desert region of rolling golden sands.

"Look," cried Maddie, pointing, "camels!" Far far below them a camel train wound its way along the edge of a chain of sand dunes.

Eventually the desert grew rather monotonous and they all dozed, dreamily content to just float along in space. Occasionally they entered banks of white cloud that reminded Maddie of cotton wool and, once, it seemed as if they flew straight into the path of the sun, while below them the cloud was like a blanket of snow, glittering and edged in gold.

At last Tariq spoke; he, along with Lyra, had been remarkably quiet throughout the journey – albeit for different reasons. "If you look down," he said, "you will see that we are leaving the desert region behind and passing over the outer fringes of the Jakabar Jungle."

Maddie peered over the edge of the carpet and saw that the golden sands of the desert far below had given way to lush green vegetation threaded with the silver strands of river tributaries. But as she did so, she felt the carpet suddenly begin to wrinkle just as it had when they had taken off. Only this time the wrinkles seemed deeper, like the furrows of a ploughed field.

Lyra's eyes snapped open. "What's the matter?" she cried. "What's happening?"

"Is there a problem?" asked Sebastian, and even he sounded anxious.

"I don't know." Tariq began chattering and Zak gave a squawk of contempt. "Something must be wrong but I don't know what it is. . ." The monkey trailed off with a gasp as the carpet suddenly rucked and buckled beneath them. "Oh dear. . .!" Frantically, he began singing the song he had sung when they had taken off but this seemed to have little effect as the carpet

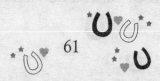

61

continued to do the strangest things: losing height, swaying, then plummeting sharply so that its passengers, even Lyra and Zak, were obliged to clutch each other in terror.

"Zak, can't you do anything?" demanded Sebastian.

"Oh, I'm in favour again, am I, when things start to go wrong?" said Zak sarcastically. "Because I'm not sure I'd do anything even if I could—"

"ZAK!" shouted Sebastian sternly.

"What do you expect me to do?" snapped the raven. "Tell me that!"

"Well, you know about flying and all that," said Maddie, her eyes like saucers as she peered fearfully over the edge. The carpet, although no longer twitching so alarmingly, was losing height fast.

"I demand you use a spell!" shrieked Lyra.

"How far are we from the end of the jungle, Tariq?" asked Sebastian.

"A very, very, very long way," chattered the monkey.

"Can't you just land?" cried Maddie.

"What, on the tops of the trees?" spluttered Tariq. "I . . . I. . ."

"Pull yourself together!" snapped Zak. "What do you think's happened to this old rag?"

"I think . . . I think . . . it's running out of magic," whispered the monkey in terror.

There was a stunned silence for a moment, then Zak gave an incredulous snort. "Think, Tariq, you've done this trip before – is there anywhere in the jungle you can land?"

"There is a clearing right in the middle," chattered the monkey, "we are just approaching it, but I fear we are going too fast."

"OK," said Zak. "In that case, I'll get behind and try to check the speed, then you'll have to bring us in to land."

"There's the clearing!" cried the monkey a few moments later and when Maddie looked down she could see the gap in the trees below.

Zak promptly flew up into the air, hovered for a moment, then, as the carpet flew past, he caught the rear-tasselled edge in his beak and pulled back with all his might. The carpet immediately jerked and slowed down.

"Right," cried the monkey, "hold tight, we're going in to land!"

Chapter Five

Deep in the Jungle

Maddie closed her eyes, too terrified to look as Tariq the monkey brought the carpet in to land. There was a whooshing sound as the wind rushed past her ears, her hair streaming out behind her, and she braced herself for the impact that would surely come as the carpet hit the ground but, somewhat surprisingly, it didn't, and when at last she dared to open her eyes it was to find that the carpet was hovering a short distance above the ground.

"Jump off, quickly," cried Tariq, "I can't keep it like this for long."

One by one the friends jumped off the carpet. Finally, Tariq himself leapt free just before the carpet wrinkled even more and fell to the ground in a crumpled, dejected heap.

Tariq hung his head in shame. Turning his back on the friends, he covered his eyes with his hands. Maddie felt sorry for him but Zak, it seemed, was unmoved. "Incompetent and inferior. Reckless too!" he spluttered.

Sebastian, however, seemed gentler. "Tell me, Tariq," he said quietly, "where did you learn your magic?"

The monkey didn't answer.

"You'd better come up with an explanation," snapped the princess, "otherwise I'll see to it that you are brought

before my father the king. He could well have you thrown into a dungeon."

This seemed to frighten the monkey even further. He turned to face them fearfully, uncovering his eyes one tiny finger at a time.

"Zoltan the Wizard." The monkey whispered so quietly that the others had to lean forward to catch what he said. "I used to work for him and I learned my magic by watching him."

"Oh *well*," snorted Zak, "that explains it!"

"Zak!" Sebastian glared at the raven.

"Let's face it," declared Zak. "If it wasn't for Zoltan and his dodgy goings-on we wouldn't all be here in the middle of this wretched jungle."

At the raven's words everyone became newly aware of their surroundings. Maddie had briefly thought that landing in the middle of a jungle might be like being in

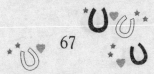

the middle of the Enchanted Forest, but apart from the fact that they were surrounded by trees, there was no resemblance. The trees in the Enchanted Forest were dark; these jungle trees were bright green with hundreds of rope-like vines looped from their branches. And there were birds, dozens of birds – parrots and parakeets and others whose names Maddie didn't know, all with brightly coloured plumage – who flitted between the trees making the most incredible noise.

"It's beautiful!" cried Maddie.

"Don't be deceived," said Sebastian warningly, as Maddie went to chase a large red butterfly. "The jungle may look beautiful, but it can also be an extremely dangerous place. We need to stay close together."

"What did he mean," said Tariq, suddenly staring at Zak, "about it being Zoltan's fault that you are all here?"

Sebastian proceeded to explain to Tariq why they had found it necessary to travel to the far side of the Jakabar Jungle. "We understand," he concluded, "that is where Zoltan now lives. Is that right?"

"I'm not s-sure," stammered the monkey, "I th-think s-o."

"What do you mean, you're not sure?" demanded Zak.

"Well, I know he used to live in the desert, but I heard he'd moved. . ."

"Do you know why?" snapped Lyra.

"No, I don't," the monkey admitted miserably.

"Presumably you need to find him as well," said Lyra.

"I . . . I . . . need to find him?" Tariq sounded terrified at the prospect.

"Well, if your magic has run out you'll need to know why, won't you? And since it's your fault we're in this mess, the least you can do is help us find Zoltan."

"I . . . I suppose so. . ." muttered Tariq miserably, as if the very thought of approaching the wizard filled him with terror.

"So you have no idea why Zoltan and his gang would have stolen Gus, and Lyra's ponies?" asked Sebastian.

Tariq shook his head. "I can't imagine."

"In that case, we'd better stop wasting time and get on and find them," said Lyra impatiently.

"So which way do we go, Tariq?" asked Maddie. She spoke gently, feeling sorry for the monkey. He seemed so distressed.

"I'm not sure," muttered Tariq, turning his head this way and that. "Let me get my bearings."

"But you do know this jungle, don't you?" asked Maddie anxiously.

"Oh yes," Tariq agreed. "I grew up here."

"Then why did you leave?" asked Zak.

"I wanted to learn magic," mumbled the monkey.

"Huh!" said Lyra. "Lot of good that did you."

"So which way?" asked Sebastian, looking around him.

"*This* way." Tariq took off suddenly, plunging through the trees and vines at a cracking pace with the others crowding behind, desperately trying to keep up.

The monkey moved so fast, half running, half swinging, that in the end Lyra called out to him to slow down. "It's all right for you," she gasped, holding her side, "you're used to all this, but I'm not."

Tariq slowed down after that, but as they fought their way through the dense jungle the sweltering heat began to affect them all.

"How much further?" grumbled Lyra.

"We're still a long way from the end of the jungle," muttered Tariq, "but I think if

71

we go just a bit further I know of somewhere we can rest a while."

They trudged on, then Maddie tugged at Sebastian's sleeve. "What is it?" he murmured so that the others wouldn't hear.

"I'm not sure," she whispered back, "but I feel as if we are being watched."

"I know," he answered out of the side of his mouth, "I feel it too, and not only that – I think we are also being followed."

"What!" Maddie squeaked and glanced fearfully over her shoulder.

"Ssh," said Sebastian warningly, "let's not alarm the others."

"But who do you think it might be?" Maddie's gaze darted from side to side, but apart from the occasional rustlings in the foliage and the calling of the birds, there was no clue.

"I've no idea," Sebastian admitted, "but don't worry – it may just be animals."

Maddie's head filled with visions of lions and tigers lying in wait.

They carried on deeper into the jungle, and then quite suddenly there was another clearing in front of them. In the centre of the clearing, half covered in vines and foliage, stood the ruins of an old stone building, its walls covered with intricate carvings. In front of the building were pillars joined by elaborate archways.

"Bless my soul!" declared Zak. "Would you look at that!"

"What is it?" Maddie asked.

"It's an old temple," replied Tariq. As they all stared in wonder, there was a sudden flurry of movement and a swarm of monkeys rushed forward and began clambering all over the ruined temple.

"Where did they come from?" declared Zak, recoiling in surprise.

"I don't like them," said Lyra warily. Some of the monkeys turned. "Oh, no,

73

they've seen us," she cried, "they're coming
this way!" The monkeys had indeed paused
in their ascent of the temple and were
studying the friends with surprised interest.
They began to descend the ruins at a rapid
pace and to lope towards Maddie and the
others, chattering and screeching as they
came.

"They're going to attack us!" cried Lyra.
"Do something, Sebastian!"

"What did you have in mind?" said Zak sarcastically.

"A spell or something. . ." wailed Lyra.

"*Another* one?" sighed Zak. "How many is that. . . ?"

By this time, Maddie was beginning to feel really frightened. The monkeys looked bigger than Tariq, as well as wilder and fiercer with pointed teeth and longer tails. "Sebastian. . ." she said urgently, "can you remember the first spell?"

"There's no need for that!" Just as the first of the monkeys had almost reached them, Tariq stepped forward and held up one hand.

"How do you know?" murmured Sebastian. He sounded anxious, as if the use of the first spell could be a real possibility.

"Because they are my cousins!" cried Tariq. "Shanka! Timba! Mol!" He stepped forward and the leading monkey stopped dead in his tracks, staring suspiciously at

Tariq. "How are you?" Tariq went on. "I haven't seen you for ages!"

"Tariq?" said the monkey incredulously, then broke into a fit of angry chattering – which several of the other monkeys joined in.

"They don't seem too pleased to see him," sniffed Lyra.

"Which means they probably won't be too pleased to welcome us," observed Zak. "Looks like you might need that spell after all, old son," he said to Sebastian.

"I need to go and talk to them," said Tariq, turning round to face the friends. "You wait here and whatever you do, don't wander off anywhere."

"As if we would," snorted Zak. "Just don't be too long, that's all."

They watched in silence as Tariq followed the other monkeys into the ruins of the old temple. "Well," said Sebastian at last, "I suppose we might as well take a

rest." With that he sat down on the ground, and after only a moment's hesitation the others joined him.

"I don't like this," said Maddie uneasily after a while, "it's starting to get dark."

"It may not be as bad as you think," said Sebastian in an attempt to reassure her.

"What do you mean!" Lyra exclaimed. "I don't see how it could get much worse. Thanks to that monkey's incompetence, we are well and truly lost in the depths of this awful jungle and surrounded by monkeys and goodness knows how many other wild animals and creepy-crawlies. Honestly, Sebastian, I don't know how you can say it might not be as bad as we think!"

"I just think we need to wait and see what Tariq has to say," said Sebastian with a shrug.

"I *demand* you use a spell," said Lyra.

"I don't want to do that yet," Sebastian replied quietly.

"I can't see why not." Lyra was getting angry. "You have two spells for goodness' sake: one to get us out of this jungle and the other for that pony's wings. I can't see what the problem is."

"And how would you propose we get home?" asked Zak suddenly. "Because there's no way that magic carpet is going to take us back to Zavania."

"We'll ride back," said Lyra, tossing her head, "on the ponies."

"It's an awfully long way," said Sebastian doubtfully.

"I've been thinking about that," said Maddie. "I was wondering how Zoltan travelled with the ponies all this way."

"He will have used magic," said Sebastian quietly, "which is why we must save some of our own."

"Uh-oh," said Zak, and they all looked up. "Tariq's coming back. Let's see what he has to say."

79

Chapter Six

The Zumi People

"Well," demanded Zak as soon as Tariq reached them, "what did they say?"

"They said we can stay the night in the temple," Tariq replied.

"I'm not sure I want to do that," declared Lyra. "It looks really creepy and I'm not sure I'd trust all those monkeys – they might attack us while we sleep."

"So you'd rather risk going on through the jungle in the dark, would you?" said Zak.

The princess fell silent and Tariq spoke up. "You would be quite safe in the temple," he said. "These are my cousins we are talking about. . ."

"But they didn't seem that pleased to see you, did they?" said Zak. "You have to admit that."

"True," Tariq agreed humbly, "they weren't pleased to see me because I left the colony and I haven't been back till now. But I'm still family and any friends of mine. . ." He trailed off.

"In that case," said Sebastian, "we'll take up their offer – thank them for us, please, Tariq."

The monkey disappeared again inside the temple. Moments later he came out and beckoned to the friends to join him.

"Oh well," said Zak, "in for a penny, in for a pound. They might even have something for us to eat."

Maddie didn't really think there was

81

much chance of that, but after the friends had crossed the clearing and entered the temple they were amazed to find that the monkeys had collected bananas, breadfruit and mangoes, which they'd placed in a circle on the floor.

"Help yourselves," said Tariq, indicating that the friends should sit down. "They'll be offended if you don't."

"Where have they gone?" asked Maddie, looking round nervously for the other monkeys.

"They won't join us," said Tariq. "They are too shy for that. But they won't be far away and they will keep watch throughout the night."

The fruit was delicious and afterwards the friends curled up on the ground to rest. Most of the roof of the temple was missing and as it grew dark Maddie watched a huge moon rise in the dark blue, star-studded sky. The birds had fallen silent but there

were many other sounds in the jungle: rustlings and the calls of animals. Maddie really didn't think she would sleep, but she felt safe under the protection of Tariq's family and when she eventually opened her eyes she was surprised to find that the sun was pouring through the open roof of the temple.

Sebastian and Zak were already awake and Maddie gently woke the princess, who was none too pleased to be roused at such an early hour.

"I'm not used to this," she grumbled. "I usually have my breakfast in bed."

"Oh, we'll have to see if we can provide room service in future," said Zak sarcastically.

"Where's that monkey?" demanded Lyra, ignoring the raven's comment.

"I don't know," said Sebastian, "we haven't seen him yet this morning. I think he spent the night with his family."

"He's lucky they are speaking to him," remarked Zak.

"I hope he comes back," said Sebastian anxiously. "We need him to lead us out of this jungle."

"He'd better," snapped Lyra. "He got us into this mess so he can jolly well get us out of it."

As if on cue, Tariq suddenly appeared in the temple entrance beneath the stone archway.

"Oh, there you are," said Lyra. "Can we go now?"

Tariq nodded. "Yes, my cousins have given me directions for the best way through the rest of the jungle."

"Did you thank them for us?" said Maddie, looking around as they left the temple. There was no sign of any monkeys.

"Of course I did," Tariq replied. He seemed strangely quiet and subdued that morning and Maddie wondered if his

84

family had completely forgiven him for leaving them in the first place.

They travelled on further and further into the dense greenness of the jungle, leaving the ruined temple and its monkeys far behind them. Tariq led the way with the princess behind him, followed by Maddie, while Sebastian and Zak brought up the rear. After a time Maddie lagged back to speak to Sebastian.

"What is it, Maddie?" he asked quietly.

"We are still being followed," she whispered. "I thought that it might have been the monkeys, but it isn't, Sebastian, I'm sure of it. So what is it? Is it other animals?" Maddie sounded frightened now.

"I don't know," said Sebastian. "We need to see if Tariq knows anything, but I don't want to cause any alarm. Tariq!" he called. "Could we stop a moment, I need a word."

The monkey stopped and waited,

chattering to himself until Sebastian and Maddie caught up.

"Tariq," said Sebastian quietly, "Maddie thinks we're being followed – and it's not your family this time."

The monkey stopped his chattering and lifted his head to listen. "Yes," he agreed at last, "I think it must be the Zumi people; they live right here in the Jakabar Jungle."

Just then Maddie looked up and gasped. Her hand flew to her mouth. "Sebastian!" she whispered. "Look!"

The others turned to where Maddie was staring and Lyra gave a squeal of fright. Just a few feet away, forming a huge circle all around them, were small people, barely taller than Maddie herself, but men, not children, with their faces daubed with paint, and spears in their hands.

Lyra was the first to recover. "Do something!" she cried, swinging round on Sebastian. "Don't just stand there!"

86

"What did you have in mind?" sniggered Zak. "Yet *another* spell?"

"If that's what it takes – yes!" snapped Lyra. "It's no good waiting until they attack us."

"I don't think they are going to attack us," said Sebastian calmly. "They live in the jungle and they simply want to know why we are here."

"Well I don't like the look of those spears," declared the princess.

"Talk to them," said Tariq. "You need to explain why you are here."

Swallowing hard, Sebastian stepped forward.

"Oh Sebastian, do be careful," Maddie begged.

"Greetings!" Sebastian raised his hand. "I understand you are the Zumi people?"

One of the men broke the circle and stepped towards Sebastian. "Who are you?" he said. "Where are you from?"

87

"My name is Sebastian," he replied. "I come from Zavania. I am a Junior WishMaster."

At his words there was much muttering amongst the Zumi tribesmen. "Who are these people with you?" asked the man who had been appointed as their spokesman.

"This is. . ." Sebastian hesitated. Then, reaching a decision, he continued, "Her Royal Highness, Princess Lyra of Zavania, and this is my friend Maddie, who is from the Other Place. This is Zak, the raven, and our guide Tariq, the monkey."

"And why are you here?" demanded the man.

"We are on a mission," Sebastian replied. "Some ponies have been stolen from Zavania and we need to get them back."

The men began muttering amongst themselves again, then the leader turned

back to the friends. "Do you know where these ponies are and who has stolen them?" he asked.

"We understand they are on the far side of the jungle and that they were stolen by Zoltan the Wizard's men."

At mention of Zoltan, the Zumi people became agitated, waving their arms about, stamping their feet and pointing their spears in a threatening manner.

"I say, steady on!" cried Zak in alarm.

"Come with us," said the leader abruptly and the friends jumped.

"We really should be getting along—" Sebastian began but he was cut short.

"You come with us," said the leader. "You must come to our village."

"What shall we do?" asked Maddie. She felt really frightened now.

"I don't think we have a choice," Sebastian replied grimly as the circle of men began to close in on them.

The Zumi people escorted the friends even deeper into the jungle until at last, just when Maddie felt she was on the point of collapsing, they reached a wide clearing and stopped. All around the clearing were ladders made of poles and ropes stretching up high into the trees.

"So where's this village then?" demanded Lyra, looking around.

"Well, bless my soul!" declared Zak, and Maddie saw that he was staring upwards. "The village is up there – they are tree dwellers – ah, people after my own heart!"

Among the leaves high above them Maddie could just make out the shapes of buildings in the branches.

"Surely we don't have to go up there!" Lyra grumbled.

"I would say that's exactly what they want us to do," said Sebastian. "And if I were you, I don't think now is the time to start arguing."

One of the men began climbing a ladder while another gestured with his spear for the friends to follow one by one. When it was her turn Maddie took a deep breath, gripped the sides of the ladder, and, without daring to look down, began climbing one rung at a time. Sebastian had gone ahead of her and when she reached the top at last he reached down, gripped her hand, and hauled her on to a platform.

Maddie paused for a moment and in wonderment gazed around her. Behind the platform was a wooden hut nestling in the branches and in the adjoining trees were other huts. Vines linked the buildings and as she watched, spellbound, Maddie caught glimpses of the Zumi people as they used the vines to swing from hut to hut. Small children played on the platforms while Zumi women sat outside preparing food and gossiping quietly with each other. All around them brightly coloured birds

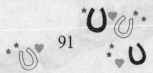

91

chattered and flitted about from branch to branch.

"Oh!" whispered Maddie, quite forgetting her fear and any danger they might still be in, "it's fantastic – a magical land!"

When the friends were all safely on the platform, one of the Zumi men escorted them inside the hut. It was dim inside, and cooler too, and when Maddie's eyes became accustomed to the gloom she saw that a man sat at one end of the hut on a sort of platform. He wore a brightly coloured robe, a tall black hat and he was smoking a white clay pipe. The Zumi guard went forward and talked urgently to the man, who stared keenly at the friends through a cloud of smoke.

"D'you reckon he's the chief?" muttered Zak.

"Yes," Sebastian agreed, "I would say so."

"Well, let's hope they're telling him I'm a princess," declared Lyra.

"Oh I expect they are," chuckled Zak. "They're probably thinking you'd fetch a good ransom."

"Zak!" said Sebastian sternly.

93

"I think they will be impressed that they have a princess visiting them," Tariq put in.

"That is what I was hoping," said Sebastian, "and that's why I told them."

"Humph! So you use the fact that I'm a princess when it suits you. . ." Lyra began crossly, but that was as far as she got, for at that moment the chief beckoned them over.

He stared at the friends for a long moment and in the silence Maddie could have sworn she could hear her knees knocking. "Welcome to our village," he said at last, and they all breathed a great sigh of relief.

"You," he said, looking directly at Sebastian, "you are a WishMaster?"

"Yes," Sebastian agreed, "but only a junior one at the moment."

"Who do you work for in Zavania?" The chief seemed more interested in Sebastian's status as a WishMaster than the fact that Lyra was a royal princess.

"I work for Zenith the WishMaster," Sebastian replied proudly.

"He's a good man," Tariq chipped in unexpectedly. "He's very highly regarded in Zavania."

"Hmm," said the chief, and after further consultation with the Zumi guard he said, "You are on a mission to free ponies from Zoltan the Wizard?"

Before Sebastian could answer Lyra stepped forward. "Three of the ponies belong to me," she said, "and it's quite disgraceful that anyone should think they could steal royal ponies and get away with it, even if he does happen to be a wizard," she added disdainfully.

"You know why Zoltan has stolen the ponies?" asked the chief. "For the same reason he steals people from our village."

"People?" gasped Maddie. "He's stolen *people*?"

"Yes," the chief replied, and nodded

solemnly. "Many people, including children, have disappeared from this village and from other Zumi villages."

"But that's terrible!" cried Maddie. "I thought it was bad enough that ponies had been stolen . . . but people . . . and even children!" She shook her head in dismay and even Lyra for once had the sense to remain silent.

"But do you know why?" asked Sebastian urgently. "Why would Zoltan want children and ponies?"

"To work," the chief replied. "To work in his mine."

"Mine?" squawked Zak in alarm. "What sort of mine? Coal mine?"

They all held their breath, waiting to hear what the chief was about to say. Instead of answering immediately, he took another long puff of his pipe, then blew a cloud of smoke across the hut. "No, not coal," he said at last.

"Then what?" said Sebastian with a frown.

"Diamonds," the chief replied. "Zoltan has a diamond mine."

Chapter Seven

The Mine

The friends gasped at his words but it was the princess who found her voice first. "Diamonds?" she said. "I say, how exciting! I like diamonds."

"Zoltan likes diamonds too," said the chief, glaring at Lyra, "but he doesn't care how he gets them. Our people are slaves digging diamonds from rock."

"And the ponies?" breathed Maddie.

"Pit ponies," said the chief, "carrying

rocks and diamonds out of the mine."

"What!" cried Lyra. "My beautiful animals used as pit ponies! I'll never be able to use them in shows again. Do something, Sebastian!"

"Here we go again. . ." muttered Zak.

"Poor little Gus will be being used for the same thing," said Maddie slowly. "He'll be frightened, just as all those poor people and ponies will be frightened. We really do have to do something, Sebastian."

"I know," said Sebastian, but he was beginning to sound worried.

"Zoltan is a very bad man," said the chief, "but he has strong magic."

"It's not *that* strong," said Tariq with a sniff. "It let me down badly."

"So what will you do?" The chief stared from one to the other.

"Sebastian has magic," said Maddie. "Good magic," she added proudly.

Sebastian took a deep breath. "Yes," he

99

agreed, "it's true I do have good magic, but it is limited. I have just two spells with me and it sounds as if I have much work to do. My assignment is to grant the wish of Gus, the flying pony who has wished that his wings would grow. Because Gus and the princess's ponies have been captured – along with your people," he added quickly – "it seems we have to find a way of rescuing them all. And as if that wasn't enough Tariq's magic has failed him, so we have to find a way of getting everyone back to Zavania."

Silence greeted his words, then Zak flapped his wings. "Easy peasy," he said, "nothing to it. I don't know what you're worried about."

"Well, I'm glad you think so, Zak," said Sebastian. "If you think it's all so easy, maybe you have some idea what we should do next."

"Actually, yes, I do," said Zak. "It's pretty

100

obvious that we need to suss out this mine of Zoltan's – see exactly where it is, that sort of thing."

Sebastian turned to the chief. "Do you know the location of the mine?"

"The mine is on the other side of river, in a deep ravine between the mountains," the chief replied.

"So how do we cross the river?" asked Sebastian.

"Over the bridge," the chief replied. "But you must take much care, or Zoltan's men will see you."

"Maybe you should stay here, Lyra," Sebastian said to the princess. "I wouldn't be able to face the king if any harm came to you."

"You can forget that," said Lyra. "I'm interested in these diamonds – I'm coming with you."

Sebastian sighed, knowing there was no point arguing with the princess when she

had her mind set on something. Turning to the chief again, he said, "Perhaps your men could take us to the bridge?"

A little while later, the friends descended from the tree-top village and in no time at all a small group of men was assembled to escort them through the jungle to the river. As they plunged into the dense greenness once more, some of the Zumi women called down imploringly to them.

"Haven't they tried to get their people back themselves?" said Lyra unsympathetically.

"Oh yes," Tariq replied. "I was talking to one of the men who told me they have tried many times but each time they have been beaten back by Zoltan's men. It will take magic to beat them, I fear – stronger magic than Zoltan's."

"Zenith's magic is the strongest of them all," said Sebastian proudly.

"Just as long as you know when to use it,

old son," cackled Zak. "And that's always supposing you can actually remember it in the first place."

"That's why I'm here," said Maddie firmly. "I can remember it."

"Thank you, Maddie," said Sebastian. "And Zak, please shut up. I don't need you constantly reminding me of what could go wrong."

Leaving the village behind, they trekked on through the jungle until the path began to rise quite steeply. "I thought we were going to cross a river," said Maddie, "so why are we climbing?"

"I don't know." Sebastian shook his head. "But I guess this bridge must be some distance away."

They climbed on and on until they found themselves high on a sort of platform of rock, with the silver gleam of a river far below them.

"So where's this bridge?" puffed Lyra.

She was clearly out of breath, hot and very bad tempered.

"The bridge is there." One of the Zumi men pointed down with his spear and cautiously the friends edged forward and peered over the edge of the platform.

"Oh my giddy aunt!" squawked Zak, while the others gasped.

There were a few steps roughly hewn out of the rock immediately below them, leading to two posts that flanked a very flimsy looking contraption constructed of ropes and narrow planks of wood which spanned the void above the river.

"For goodness' sake," said Lyra crossly, "that's ridiculous! You can't expect me to cross on that! I'm a royal princess, in case you've forgotten."

"Fat chance of that," muttered Zak.

"Is there really no other way over?" asked Sebastian, turning to one of the Zumi men.

The man shook his head. "This is the only way."

"You don't have to come," said Zak to the princess. "You can always stay here. You might miss a few diamonds but. . ."

"It's all right for you," snapped Lyra, "you can always fly over."

"Stop squabbling," said Sebastian firmly. "No one has to cross on the bridge if they don't want to. They can wait here until we come back." He paused and glanced around him. "Where's Tariq?"

"I don't know," said Maddie. "He was here just now."

"The monkey has gone," said one of the Zumi men. "He went off into the jungle."

"He's chickened out!" said Zak in disgust.

"Well, let's hope that's all it is," said Lyra.

"What do you mean?" Sebastian stared at her.

Lyra shrugged. "Didn't he say he used to work for Zoltan? It's my bet he's gone to warn him we're on our way."

"He wouldn't!" cried Maddie. "Would he, Sebastian?" she added uncertainly.

"Well, we hope he wouldn't," said Sebastian, "but whatever the reason, the fact is he's gone so we'll just have to press on without him."

Leaving the Zumi people behind, the friends prepared to cross the bridge. Maddie didn't think she'd ever felt so frightened in her life as she stepped on to the wooden planks of the bridge and, holding on to the ropes, slowly began to walk forward. Lyra came behind her and as she stepped on to the bridge the extra weight made it sway alarmingly. The princess gave a screech of alarm and Maddie jumped in fright, almost losing her footing on the slippery planks.

"Quiet!" called Sebastian from the rear.

"We don't want to draw attention to ourselves in case any of Zoltan's men are around."

Slowly, while Zak hovered alongside, the friends made their way across the bridge one step at a time until, just when all seemed to be going well, the princess suddenly stopped. "I can't!" she said. "I can't go any further!"

Maddie half-turned, still holding on tightly to the ropes. "Yes, you can," she said. "We're halfway there. It's not much further. Don't look down," she added, as Lyra peered over the rope.

"Look!" whimpered Lyra. "Look down there. Those rocks!"

Maddie glanced down to where, far below, the water swirled around some jagged, fearsome-looking rocks. "Hold on to my hand," she said firmly to Lyra.

The princess nervously held out her hand and gripped Maddie's, then the two girls cautiously inched their way across the flimsy, swaying bridge until, after what seemed like a lifetime, they reached the other side and stepped thankfully on to firm land. Moments later they were joined by Sebastian and Zak, who swooped in to join them.

After a short rest the friends set off up the narrow, rocky path that led to the

108

mountain pass, following directions given to them by the Zumi people. The path grew steeper and steeper, much steeper than the path up to Edgar's Eyrie, and Maddie found herself wishing they were back there in Zavania instead of here in this wild and dangerous place. But they had work to do: there wasn't just a wish to grant, for many people were in trouble and now they must find the best way for their magic to help them.

As they reached the top of the pass, Sebastian called a halt. "We need to rest," he said, "before we go down into the ravine. But before that – Zak, you have a job to do."

"Yeah, yeah, I know," sighed Zak. "You're going to send me in first to suss things out."

"Right first time," said Sebastian, as they all peered down into the deep ravine.

It was a wild and rocky place with very

little sign of life, but far below them, against one side of the rock face, was a large wooden structure surrounded by what looked like huge cattle pens.

"Look," breathed Maddie. "There are animals in those pens and they look like ponies!"

"My ponies!" cried the princess. She'd been very quiet since crossing the river but the sight of the ponies in the pens had stirred her up again.

"So do you think that's the mine?' Maddie asked.

"Almost certainly," Sebastian replied. "You can see an opening like the mouth of a cave in the rock face just beside those wooden buildings. And look, there are more ponies and they are pulling carts. . ."

"Full of diamonds?" asked Lyra, her eyes sparkling.

"They just look like old rocks to me," sniffed Zak.

110

"Well, they would," said Sebastian. "They would need to be cut and polished before they look like diamonds." He paused, then after a moment said, "I believe Zoltan's recent visit to Zavania was purely and simply to steal ponies since there are no ponies in the jungle. . . Zak, you go down and have a look around before we go any further. We don't want to go slap-bang into Zoltan or his men."

"All right, all right, I'm going," said Zak.

"Do be careful, Zak," said Maddie anxiously.

"Course I will," said the raven. He flapped his wings a couple of times then took off and glided down into the ravine as his friends watched.

Chapter Eight

Diamonds!

They waited a long time for Zak to return, but there was no sign of that reassuring black shape swooping in to land.

"So where's he got to?" demanded Lyra.

"He'll be back soon," said Sebastian. "Zak always comes back." But by this time even he was beginning to sound a little anxious.

The sky began to darken. "I don't like the look of those black clouds," said

Maddie. "I think it might be going to rain."

"It's so hot," complained Lyra, "it feels as if we might be about to have a storm."

They waited a while longer but when there was still no sign of Zak Sebastian stood up. "We can't wait any more," he said. "We need to go down there ourselves and see what is happening. We may have to split up later, but for the time being we should stay close."

Very cautiously they began to climb down into the ravine, stopping every so often and taking cover behind clumps of rocks in case anyone was watching out for intruders. They had almost reached the bottom of the ravine when there came a rumble of thunder in the distance.

"I don't like storms," muttered Lyra.

"Neither do I," said Maddie.

At last, under cover of a particularly large rock, they were able to observe the

mine and the structures surrounding it. To one side of the entrance to the cave there was a wooden tripod with a large wheel with ropes attached. "That would be for drawing the rocks up out of the mine," murmured Sebastian.

"Look at those wooden cages!" whispered Maddie and they all turned to see where she was looking. "There are people inside them – oh, Sebastian!" Her hand flew to her mouth. "It's the Zumi people!" The cage-like structures were indeed packed with people, their hands and thin arms poking out pathetically through the bars as the short squat figure of a guard strutted up and down in front of them.

"It's Boris," muttered Sebastian. "I'd know him anywhere – he stayed in the East Tower during Zoltan's visit."

"He looks a real brute." Maddie shuddered.

"He is," said Sebastian grimly.

Lyra poked her head out from behind the rock. "So where are my ponies?" she demanded.

"Be careful," warned Sebastian. "The cattle pens are over there. . . Oh, wait a minute, something is happening. . ." As they watched, a line of ponies came out of the entrance of the cave. Each of them was straining to draw separate carts filled to the brim with what looked like chunks of rock.

"That's Blaze!" the princess hissed as the first of the ponies passed close to where the friends were hiding. "He's one of my ponies!"

"And there's Gus," breathed Sebastian, as the second pony passed by. He was white, with a beautiful coloured mane and tail and little lumps on his back where his wings should have been. He looked very sad and dejected and Maddie noticed that a single tear trickled down his nose as he strained to pull the heavy cart.

"Poor things," whispered Maddie. "We have to do something, Sebastian."

"Yes, I know we do," he agreed grimly, "but first I want to find Zak and to know where Zoltan is."

"Look at that!" Maddie tugged at Sebastian's sleeve. A line of Zumi people, some of them children, were being led out of the mine by another guard.

"Wulfric!" breathed Sebastian. The friends watched as the guard pushed and shoved the people into the wooden cages. They appeared thin and underfed and were dressed in nothing more than tattered rags.

"I want to see inside the mine," said Sebastian quietly. "If we are very careful we can creep along behind the cages and slip inside. Come on, keep close together."

In single file and under cover of the rocks they ran, bent almost double, behind the cages and into the cave. Here they

followed a tunnel-like passage that led into a huge cavern.

The sight before them almost took their breath away. The Zumi people were everywhere, toiling long and hard as they filled carts with the rocks that were being hoisted to the surface in large leather buckets. The carts themselves were pulled away by yet more ponies, who struggled to haul heavy loads that, in some cases, were bigger than themselves.

"We mustn't be seen," whispered Sebastian, "otherwise we'll find ourselves prisoners as well and will be digging out rocks for the rest of our lives."

Maddie clutched his arm. "There's Zoltan!" she whispered. The wizard had appeared on a ledge on the far side of the cavern and, dressed in his long red robes, his arms folded, was surveying the scene before him.

"*Use a spell*," muttered Lyra furiously.

"Honestly, Sebastian, I don't know what you're waiting for."

"He has Zak!" gasped Maddie in sudden alarm. "Look, on his arm!"

"What!" spluttered Sebastian. They all looked and sure enough, there was Zak on the wizard's arm – a very despondent-looking Zak, with his wings held limply at

his sides and his head hanging down.

"Why doesn't he just fly away, the stupid bird?" sniffed Lyra.

"He's tied on," breathed Maddie. "Look – there's a chain round his leg and it's attached to the wizard's belt."

"If Zoltan's harmed him. . ." muttered Sebastian.

"Poor Zak!" said Maddie. "Sebastian, we must do something. *Now*."

"Oh, so it's a different story where that wretched bird is concerned, is it?" snapped Lyra. "You weren't too bothered when it was my ponies, were you?"

"Of course we were!" Maddie's eyes flashed. "Sebastian wants to rescue *everyone*, but it's dangerous."

"It is indeed," said Sebastian, and although he spoke quietly there was an edge to his voice. "Now that Zoltan has Zak he will be on his guard, as he will suspect Zak has not come alone." He

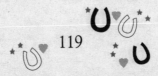

119

paused. "Listen, this is what we are going to do. I will go to the back of the cages, where hopefully I won't be seen, then I'll talk to some of the Zumi people and tell them that they must be ready because we are about to attempt a rescue operation. Maddie, I want you and Lyra to go to the animal pens, find Gus and the royal ponies and tell them to be ready and to alert the other ponies. But remember – take great care that you are not seen."

Moments later, Sebastian crept out from the cave and crawled behind the cages where the Zumi people were imprisoned while Maddie and Lyra made their way across to the cattle pens, running from rock to rock.

There were a lot of ponies in the pens and the animal smell was almost overpowering. For a moment the two girls didn't quite know where to go first, then Maddie suddenly caught sight of the little

white pony that she'd earlier seen pulling a cart. "Gus!" she whispered urgently and when he didn't appear to hear her she tried again, a little louder. "Gus!"

The pony lifted his head and, staring towards the back of the pen, caught sight of Maddie and Lyra. Immediately he trotted across, whickering gently.

"Who are you?" he murmured, after glancing over his shoulder in fear to make sure none of Zoltan's guards were around.

"I'm Maddie, I'm a friend of Sebastian the WishMaster," Maddie replied.

"Sebastian?" Gus's eyes rolled and his nostrils flared. "Is he here?"

"Yes, he is," Maddie replied. Turning to Lyra, she said, "this is the Princess Lyra, Gus. Some of her ponies were captured at the same time as you."

Gus nodded. "They are over there." He jerked his head. "Have you come to

rescue us?" he asked. "It'll be very difficult – there are heavy chains on all the gates."

"Sebastian has magic," whispered Maddie.

"Oh, thank goodness!" cried Gus joyfully. "I thought we'd all be here for ever!"

"But you need to be ready to run when the time comes," Maddie warned urgently.

"You must warn my ponies as well," said the princess.

"And *all* the other ponies," Maddie added.

"How will we know when the time comes?" asked Gus. He sounded anxious.

"You will know," Maddie replied reassuringly. "Never fear – just be ready." Reaching out her hand, she touched the little pony's velvety nose. "We must go now."

"Just a minute," said Lyra. "Where were

you taking the diamond rocks in those carts?" she asked Gus.

"To Zoltan's barge down on the river," Gus replied.

At that moment there came a large clap of thunder almost directly overhead and the two girls dived for cover again behind the rocks. There they found Sebastian waiting for them.

"Did you see Gus?" he asked.

"Yes," Maddie replied. "He knows you are here and that he and the other ponies have to be ready for the rescue operation. What about the Zumi people?"

"They know as well," Sebastian said grimly. "I only hope they will have the strength to run."

"Zoltan has a lot to answer for," said Maddie.

"He does," Sebastian agreed.

"But what about Zak?" asked Maddie fearfully, as further rolls of thunder

rumbled around the ravine. "How will he know to be ready?"

"Zak will know," said Sebastian. "Don't worry. Did Gus say anything about his wish?"

Maddie shook her head. "I think he was more concerned about being held prisoner."

"That may be so, but I still have to grant his wish," Sebastian replied.

Lyra gaped at them in astonishment. "Now, hang on a minute," she said, "surely you're not *still* going to waste one of your spells on that ridiculous wish?"

"Of course I am," Sebastian replied quietly. "Let's not forget that our whole reason for being here is because of Gus's wish."

"That may well be," Lyra declared hotly, "but that was then – things have changed. It seems to me you'll need every scrap of your magic to release everyone from that

mad wizard's clutches and get us – and the diamonds – back to Zavania."

"You are quite right in that I need to release everyone," said Sebastian. "Not only Gus and the ponies, but the Zumi people, and of course Zak . . . however, I also have to carry out the terms of my assignment, which means I must grant Gus's wish."

Watching him, Maddie felt a lump in her throat.

"So how do you propose we get home?" demanded Lyra.

"We'll have to find another way," said Sebastian calmly. "Now, if no one has any further objections, I suggest we mount this rescue operation."

"What do you want me to do?" asked Maddie.

"Say the first spell with me, Maddie," he replied.

"Right," said Maddie taking a deep

breath, "the first spell. . ."

Together, she and Sebastian, watched by Lyra, began to recite the first of the two spells they had so carefully written in the turret room.

>"*Jezophat and Jallodeer,*
>*Engulf us in your Fire.*
>*Judefer under Jaxoper,*
>*Bring Power through Sapphire!*"

As they finished the spell, Sebastian lifted the hand bearing the ring with its deep blue sapphire stone. In the silence, in a voice both steady and calm, he said, "Through the magic of the Sapphire, release all the prisoners and collapse the mine."

Chapter Nine

The Rescue

As they waited, complete and utter silence fell upon the ravine. Even the thunder subsided. In the stillness, a strong blue light suddenly flashed several times high above them, before bathing the entire ravine in its strange light. Then, as abruptly as it had come, the light dimmed and disappeared.

"Nothing's happening," hissed Lyra. "It hasn't worked."

"Of course it has," said Maddie indignantly. "Just be patient."

They waited again, then Lyra gasped. "Oh, look!" she said, lifting her head and peering out from behind the rock. "Just look at that!"

The others turned, craning their necks, as the wooden slates forming the cages where the Zumi people were imprisoned began creaking and shuddering, before falling to the ground with an enormous crash. There was a further moment of silence, then the people inside began to surge forward, yelling in delight at their freedom.

At the same time the chains and poles forming the animal pens also fell and the ponies first began to trot from the pens, then to canter, then to stampede through the ravine to freedom.

Some of Zoltan's men ran from the cave and made a feeble attempt to stop them

but were beaten back by the sheer numbers.

A low rumbling sound filled the air and at first Maddie thought it was more thunder, but as it grew louder and louder and even more people and ponies began to emerge from the cave, she realized it was the mine itself that was about to collapse.

"Sebastian!" she cried. "Where is Zak?"

Sebastian looked round wildly for his friend but there was no sign of that familiar black shape, and fear gripped Maddie as she wondered what on earth Sebastian would do without the raven. Then he gave a great shout. "Here he comes!" he cried, and the relief in his voice was only too obvious as the raven flew out of the cave and up into the air, before swooping down to land on Sebastian's shoulder. "Thank goodness you're safe," he said.

"And not before time." Zak was clearly indignant. "You've no idea what I've been

through. Why, at one point there I thought—"

"Yes, all right, Zak," said Sebastian, "at least you're OK now. You can tell us all about it later, but first I need to know – where is Zoltan?"

"I don't know." Zak shook his head. "Last I saw of him was when my chains suddenly fell off and the rumbling started in the mine. What's going to happen to it, old son?"

"It is going to collapse when all the prisoners are safe," Sebastian replied.

"Good strategy," said Zak admiringly.

At that moment, Gus and three other ponies broke away from the rest of the herd and galloped across to the friends. Lyra immediately began patting and petting her ponies. She put her arms around Blaze's neck and hugged him while Maddie did the same to little Gus. "I'm so pleased you are safe," she said, and the little pony nuzzled her shoulder in gratitude.

The rumbling from the mine grew much louder, the ground began to tremble and the structures around the cave began to shake.

"Shiver me timbers!" muttered Zak and promptly tucked his head under his wing while the rest of the friends, including the ponies, huddled together.

The rumbling and shaking rose to a ear-splitting crescendo and great clouds of dust billowed from the entrance to the cave, but gradually the noise grew less and less until eventually it stopped altogether.

"Where have the Zumi people gone?" asked Maddie, looking around her.

"I told them once they were free to run for the bridge," said Sebastian, "and the other ponies will eventually make their own way back to their herds."

"What about Zoltan?" asked Maddie.

"Do you think he will have got out of the mine before it collapsed?" She gave a little shudder.

"You can depend on that," said Sebastian grimly. "And his men will have scattered if they know what's good for them."

"So where is Zoltan?" asked Lyra, nervously looking over her shoulder.

"I saw him," said Gus suddenly and they all turned to look at the little pony. "He ran out of the mine with his men just before it collapsed. He'll have gone down to the river to his barge, which is packed with the diamonds – he won't want to lose *them*."

"I don't think he should be allowed to get away with them," sniffed Lyra. As she spoke, she reached behind a rock and hauled out a bulging sack that she'd obviously been hiding there.

"Where on earth did you get that?" asked Maddie in amazement.

"I found it on the ground inside the cave," Lyra replied. "And I managed to grab some of the rocks. But Zoltan must have *hundreds* of diamonds! It's a disgrace!"

"I know," said Sebastian. "After granting Gus's wish, I will have to face Zenith and tell him about Zoltan." A worried frown crossed his features. "That could be tricky, bearing in mind the two of them are friends."

"Well, they were before all this happened," said Maddie. "I doubt Zenith will be too happy when he hears what has gone on."

"That's neither here nor there," said Lyra crossly. "The issue is that Zoltan is going to escape with all those diamonds and I think he should be stopped."

"There's nothing we can do about it now," said Sebastian. "In the meantime, what we can do is to start our journey back to Zavania. If we hurry, we can get back

across the bridge and make our way to the Zumi village before nightfall. But before that – Gus, I'm going to grant your wish. Are you ready, Maddie?"

"Oh yes."

"Are you ready, Gus?"

The little pony nodded and Maddie thought he was so choked up he was unable to speak.

And so, for the second time that day, Sebastian and Maddie began to recite a spell together:

> *"Jostephar of Jilliban,*
> *Raise Flame of Deepest Blue,*
> *Jarredome and Janzebar,*
> *Bring Magic Sure and True."*

When they had finished, Sebastian lifted his hand and said in a loud voice, "Sapphire, send your magic and give Gus his wings."

This time they were all ready for the flash of blue but it was gentler than before, a soft blue light that hovered over the ravine like an early morning mist.

Everyone turned to look at Gus as slowly, very slowly, the bumps on his back began to grow.

"Wow!" gasped Maddie. "Just look at that!"

The bumps had grown into long spines and beautiful, feathered, rainbow-coloured wings began to unfurl.

Maddie clasped her hands. "Oh Gus, your wings are amazing!"

"But will he be able to fly?" asked Lyra. "He hasn't had lessons like the others."

"I listened to everything that Rupert told them," said Gus, "so I think I could try."

"Let's see it then," said Lyra.

"There will be plenty of time for that later," said Sebastian. "I think we should go now; I still don't trust Zoltan."

The friends needed no further encouragement and they all began to move through the ravine towards the mountain pass.

Gus trotted forward so that he was between Sebastian and Maddie. "Thank you so much for granting my wish and making my wings grow."

"That's all right, Gus," Sebastian replied. "Our work is done now, but I won't rest until everyone is safely home in Zavania."

They all scrambled up the pass, with one last backward glance down into the ravine at the cloud of dust that still hung in the air around the mine and the heaps of wood from the cages and the animal pens. Then they pushed onwards through the narrow pathway to the bridge.

"I'm not looking forward to this bit," admitted Maddie as the first glimpse of the bridge came into view.

"Neither am I," grumbled Lyra. "I still think you should have used that last spell to get us all home. I'm sure Zenith would have found another spell for the wings. I really don't like this bridge and I don't think it's right I should be expected to cross it again."

In spite of the princess's protests, Maddie could not help noticing that she was still dragging along the bag of diamond rocks that she'd rescued from the mine.

In single file, the friends, the princess, Gus and the other ponies made their way carefully across the flimsy bridge, which swayed and creaked under their combined weight.

When they were halfway across, a sudden shout from Zak – who was flying alongside – made them all freeze. "What's that?" he cried. For coming towards the bridge on the river below was a boat; a long flat barge that looked as if it was packed with a bulky cargo. Three men could quite clearly be seen at the prow.

"It's Zoltan!" cried Gus, his eyes rolling in fear.

"Quickly!" shouted Sebastian. "Get to the other side."

"What can he do?" shouted Lyra. "He's down there and we're up here."

"He still has magic, don't forget, and he won't be happy at what we've done."

At Sebastian's words, everyone quickened their pace and by the time the barge and its occupants reached the bridge the friends had all gained the safety of the other side.

"I wouldn't have put it past Zoltan to have destroyed the bridge with us on it," muttered Sebastian as they took cover in the dense jungle foliage.

"I *still* don't think he should be allowed to get away, and especially with all those diamonds," grumbled Lyra.

138

"I'm afraid we don't have any way of stopping him now," said Sebastian, and Maddie could not help hearing the regret in his voice. But then, just when it seemed that Zoltan and his men would get away with their cargo, there was a flurry of movement in the dense jungle foliage and a small figure rushed on to the bridge, closely followed by dozens of other figures.

"Bless my soul!" cried Zak. "It's Tariq and his monkey chums!"

As the friends watched in astonishment, the monkeys began to hurl rocks from the bridge down on to the barge. They were quickly joined by dozens of other monkeys, who lined the river bank and also flung stones and rocks at the vessel bearing Zoltan and his bodyguards.

"So he didn't desert us," breathed Maddie, "I didn't think he would."

Under the barrage of missiles the barge

began to shudder and shake and sprang several leaks, but in spite of the onslaught it continued on its journey up the river.

"It needs something else to sink it," muttered Zak.

"But we don't have anything else," Maddie said in desperation.

"Yes we do!" cried Gus. Before anyone could stop him, the little pony lowered his head and picked up Lyra's bag of diamond rocks from the ground with his teeth. Before everyone's startled gaze, he flapped his new, beautiful, rainbow wings a couple of times, then rose up into the air.

"Oh my giddy aunt!" cried Zak. "Where's he going?"

"He has my diamonds!" cried Lyra in dismay. "Stop him, Sebastian!"

But there was no stopping Gus. He flew strongly out over the river, following the barge until he was directly above it, and then, carefully positioning himself, he

dropped the sack of rocks from a great height fairly and squarely on to the vessel.

The barge shuddered and shook again. "I say, good shot!" Zak shouted in delight.

The impact had the desired effect. In no time at all the boat appeared to have sprung a large leak and started to founder, while Zoltan and his men began yelling and shouting in alarm. Watched by the friends on the path high above the river, and by the monkeys who cheered and danced up and down in glee, the barge steadily filled with water and began to sink until at last, in desperation, Zoltan – quickly followed by Boris and Wulfric – dived into the water and began to swim to the far bank.

With a final gurgle the barge with its cargo of diamonds slid beneath the water. "What a terrible waste!" raged Lyra. "And my diamonds too!"

"At least Zoltan hasn't got away with any diamonds," said Sebastian. As Gus

flew back to join them, they all (with the exception of Lyra) applauded the little pony. "Well done, Gus," Sebastian said, "that was very quick thinking and brave of you. And you can fly brilliantly, in spite of not having had any lessons."

Gus was overcome with embarrassment. "Like I said, I listened very carefully to Rupert when he was teaching the others," he mumbled.

A moment later Tariq ran to join the friends, who also showered him with thanks and praise.

"I wanted to do something to help!" said Tariq. "But I must say," he added admiringly, "I didn't think your magic would be so powerful. I brought the monkeys to help with the rescue but now I'm not sure you needed them."

"Your friends must have weakened the barge," said Maddie, "and then Gus here was able to finish it off."

"I say, look at that lot over there on the rocks," chortled Zak, and the friends all turned to look at the wizard and his men. "Where do you think they'll go now, Sebastian?"

"I don't know," said Sebastian, "I wouldn't put anything past Zoltan—" But that was as far as he got, for at that moment the sky darkened dramatically.

"Oh dear," said Maddie in alarm, "I think the storm's coming back. Either that or Zoltan's trying some magic." Even as she spoke, there was a huge flash of forked lightning that lit up the whole sky, followed almost immediately by a deafening clap of thunder, which caused the friends to huddle together in fright.

Maddie was the first to look up and what she saw made her cry out in utter amazement. "Look!" she cried. "Look, there on the bridge!"

Zak came out from under his wing and

Tariq peered round Sebastian's cloak and they all stared in astonishment, for there on the bridge was a tall figure dressed in black.

"Zenith!" breathed Sebastian.

Chapter Ten

The End of the Adventure

"Jeepers!" muttered Zak. "What's *he* doing here?"

"I don't know," admitted Sebastian worriedly. "I've never known him to appear during an assignment before."

"Well, it looks like we're about to find out," said Zak out of the side of his beak.

But Zenith didn't seem interested in the friends; instead, his attention seemed to be on the bedraggled figures scrambling about on the rocks on the far side of the river. When he spoke, his voice was loud and authoritative. "Zoltan!"

"Here we go. . ." said Zak. "This should teach 'em!"

"Don't forget they've been friends for years," said Sebastian, sounding more worried than ever.

The figure in red on the rocks froze, then turned and peered up at the bridge, his two companions doing likewise.

"Zoltan," Zenith's voice rang out, "you are a disgrace to your profession."

"Zenith. . ." Zoltan held out his arms to his friend, but Zenith remained unmoved, standing on the bridge with his legs apart and his arm folded.

"I am here by authority of the King of Zavania," Zenith declared.

"*Now* we're getting somewhere," said Lyra smugly.

"Your recent behaviour," Zenith

146

continued, "has fallen far short of that expected of a royal wizard. I have been commanded by the king to strip you of your magic powers."

"No, Zenith, no!" Zoltan was clearly agitated now, and Boris and Wulfric looked absolutely terrified.

"Furthermore," Zenith continued, while the friends held their breath, "you need to be punished for bringing fear and terror to those less fortunate than yourself. That is not what we do, Zoltan, and that is not why we are given magic powers."

"That's right," Zak muttered, "you tell 'em, Zenith."

"By the powers vested in me," the wizard announced, "the three of you will be banished to the far north, where you will be engaged in hard labour in the Salt Mines until the king sees fit to release you."

"No, Zenith, no! Not the Salt Mines,"

147

cried Zoltan. "Anything but the Salt Mines! It's cold in the north and miserable. . ." But that was as far as he got, for Zenith raised his right hand.

"So be it!" he said.

The sky darkened again and there was a further flash of lightning.

"Look!" Tariq cried, pointing towards the rocks. "They've disappeared!"

And they had. The space where Zoltan, Boris and Wulfric had been cowering on the rocks was now empty and there was not even a ripple on the river to show where the barge full of diamonds had sunk. As they watched, Zenith turned and walked towards them across the bridge.

"Now for the moment of truth!" Zak murmured.

"Shut up, Zak," said Sebastian, rubbing his palms down the side of his breeches, "it's bad enough without your comments."

The WishMaster stepped off the bridge

148

and Sebastian took a step forward to greet him. "Zenith," he said, and although his voice sounded steady Maddie knew he was uneasy.

"Sebastian." Zenith nodded, and turning to Lyra gave a little bow. "Your Royal Highness." Then he turned back to Sebastian. "You've done well," he proclaimed. "Your assignment has been difficult, but you have conducted yourself as befits your position."

"I thought you would be angry," Sebastian admitted, "because Zoltan was your friend."

"He was my friend once," Zenith agreed, "but not any more. He has abused our friendship and used his powers in the most despicable ways."

"But how did you know what was happening?" said Maddie as curiosity got the better of her.

"When the king and queen and I

returned to Zavania," said Zenith, "it was to find that the Princess Lyra and yourselves were pursuing Gus and the princess's ponies. This was all right as far as I was concerned until I found out about Zoltan's involvement from Edgar. I have to say, it didn't come as such a shock as it once might have done because I'd become suspicious of Zoltan during his visit."

"Had you?" Sebastian asked faintly.

Zenith nodded. "He'd grown very greedy and could talk about nothing but amassing a fortune – and that is not what we wizards are about. As soon as I heard what had happened I knew that you could all be in deadly danger and that you might not have enough magic with you to deal with the situation."

"Seems like he cares about us after all," murmured Zak.

"I had already decided to intervene," Zenith continued, "when the king

commanded me to find the princess and bring her back safely to Zavania. I have to say, though, you seem to have coped remarkably well."

"Did you know about the diamond mines?" asked Lyra.

Zenith nodded. "I spoke with the chief of the Zumi people and he told me all that had happened. They are overjoyed to have their people returned to them."

"We've lost a mine full of diamonds though," said Lyra peevishly.

"That does not matter," Zenith replied. "The diamonds have returned to the ground from whence they came. That is how it should be." Now his gaze fell upon Gus. "And you've had your wish granted, which really was the whole object of this exercise. All that remains now is for you all to return to Zavania."

"There is just one other thing," said Sebastian, "and that is our friend, Tariq."

He turned to the monkey. "Tariq worked for Zoltan and learned some magic, but his powers failed and we had to abandon his magic carpet. Tariq, however, remained loyal to us and with the help of his monkey family has helped us carry out the assignment."

Zenith looked at the monkey. "Would you like me to restore your powers?" he asked.

"Thank you, Zenith," said the monkey, "but actually, the thing I would like more than anything else is to return to my family. I should never have left them in the first place."

"Very well." Zenith nodded, and Tariq turned to say a tearful farewell to the friends.

"Goodbye, Tariq," said Maddie, hugging the little monkey. "I'll never forget you."

"Nor I you," sniffed Tariq.

Even Zak and Lyra seemed sad to see

the monkey go as, with a backward glance and a wave of one tiny hand, he disappeared back into the jungle with the crowd of chattering monkeys.

Zenith called for their attention again. "Now," he said, "Gus and Zak will both fly home to Zavania, and the rest of you will take a pony each and ride back."

"It's an awfully long way," said Sebastian, looking doubtfully at the ponies.

"I will use a spell," said Zenith. "I promise you it will not take you as long as you think."

"But I can't ride," whispered Maddie, suddenly frightened at the thought of the journey ahead.

"Oh," said Zenith, "I think you'll find you can. . ."

"I shall ride Blaze," announced Lyra, and quickly mounted her favourite pony.

Sebastian held out his hand to Maddie.

153

"Come on," he said kindly, "I'll help you to mount – don't forget, you've ridden unicorns before."

"I know," said Maddie, "but I was holding on to you then."

"I don't think these ponies could carry two of us," said Sebastian as he helped her up on to the back of one of the other ponies. "Don't worry, Maddie," he murmured, just before he walked away to his own mount, "Zenith's magic will have taken care of everything."

The pony, whose name was Spirit, began to move beneath her and Maddie clung on to his mane for dear life, but as he gathered speed she felt herself relax. Even though she knew it was Zenith's magic helping her, she was surprised that riding felt so natural. Within no time at all she found herself enjoying the journey as they all rode like the wind back to Zavania.

*

154

When they arrived in the paddock behind the royal mews Maddie was almost disappointed – she'd enjoyed the ride so much that she'd wanted it to go on for ever. As she slid from the pony's back, she patted his nose and thanked him for

155

bringing her back to Zavania.

Maddie looked around her and realized there was no sign of Zenith.

"He will have gone straight to report to the king," said Sebastian.

"Well, my ponies," said Lyra, "at last you are back where you belong. Off you go!" Whinnying with delight, the three ponies kicked up their heels and cantered off across the paddock.

"I must go and speak to my parents," said Lyra. She turned away, and for one moment Maddie thought she wasn't even going to say goodbye. But then she turned back. "Thank you," she said to no one in particular, "for helping me find my ponies." And with a toss of her head, she was gone.

"That's all we're likely to get out of *her*," sniffed Zak. "What about you, Gus – what are you going to do next?"

"I'm going to go down to the far

paddock and see Rupert," Gus replied. "I know I can fly, but I'm sure there are some tips he will want to give me. After that I will fly to join the rest of my herd." He paused, and looked from Sebastian to Zak and then to Maddie. "I will never forget you," he said, "and what you have done for me. If there is ever anything I can do to help you, you only have to say the word."

"We shall miss you, Gus," said Maddie as she put her arms around the little pony and hugged him.

Moments later Gus took to the air and flew gracefully down to the far paddock, where they could just see the figure of Rupert waiting for him.

"Well, that's that then," said Zak. "End of another successful assignment."

"Yes," Sebastian agreed, "and all we need to do now, Maddie, is to take you home."

157

It was dark and quiet beneath the willows, but the sound of music and laughter was drifting down the garden from the house.

"The barbecue!" whispered Maddie. "I'd forgotten all about that. Oh, I do wish you two could come."

"So do we," said Sebastian quietly.

"Yes," agreed Zak, "I'm quite partial to a bit of steak."

"Never mind," said Maddie with a sigh as Sebastian helped her from the boat. "I just hope that it won't be too long before someone else makes a wish."

"And when they do," said Sebastian, "you can be sure we will be straight back here to collect you."

"Goodbye, Sebastian . . . goodbye, Zak." Maddie had to bite her lip to stop it trembling.

"Goodbye, Maddie," they called in unison. "Thank you for your help," Sebastian added. And then they were

gone, leaving only ripples on the surface of the water.

Still biting her lip, Maddie turned and made her way up the garden. She was unable to prevent a tear that spilled out of her eye and trickled down her cheek.

She met her mother on the patio. "Oh, there you are," her mother said. "Jessica and her family have just arrived. Jessica has been riding, apparently." She paused. "Are you *sure* you wouldn't like to go riding, Maddie?" she asked.

"Do you know," said Maddie thoughtfully, thinking of Gus and Spirit and that wonderful ride out of Jakabar, "I think I might – it could be fun."

"Well, we'll have to see if we can arrange it," said her mother before she hurried off to welcome some more guests.

And it *could* be fun, thought Maddie – especially seeing Jessica's face when she realized that Maddie could ride after all.

Even better, it would be something to do while she waited for someone else to make a wish. With a little sigh, she turned just as her friend Lucy came out on to the patio. "Hi, Lucy," she said.

"Hi, Maddie," said Lucy. "I wondered where you were. I came out here just a moment ago and I couldn't find you."

"Oh, I'd only popped down the garden for a minute," said Maddie. "That's all." She wondered what her friend would say if she really knew where she'd been and the exciting adventures she'd had, but she knew she could never tell her about that other land, just as Sebastian and Zak could never join them in her world.

But as she caught the mouth-watering smell of the barbecue, she realized people were dancing to the music of her favourite pop group. Suddenly, in spite of her sadness at not being able to share all the wonderful things of Zavania, Maddie felt happy to be

160

home once more, with her family and friends all around her.

Unicorn Wishes

*In the magical land of Zavania, an unhappy
unicorn has made a wish…*

A baby unicorn has been taken away
from his mother and kept in the royal
castle as Princess Lyra's pet. Now he's
made a wish to go home, but nobody
knows where that is!

Sebastian and his friends Maddie and
Zak are determined to help. Their quest
takes them deep into the Enchanted
Forest, where a dangerous magic is
lying in wait. . .

Mermaid Wishes

*In the magical land of Zavania, a frightened
mermaid has made a wish. . .*

Seraphina is desperately ill, almost dying.
Her beautiful golden hair is tangled and
matted, and without her own enchanted
comb she will never recover. She has
wished for it back. But who took it?
Where is it now?

Sebastian, Maddie and Zak must find the
comb, and grant the mermaid's wish.
And they must find it quickly, for
Seraphina is fading fast. . .